Denationalisation
of Money
—*The Argument Refined*

An Analysis of the Theory
and Practice of Concurrent Currencies

F. A. HAYEK
Nobel Laureate 1974

Diseases desperate grown,
By desperate appliances are reli'ved,
Or not at all.
WILLIAM SHAKESPEARE
(*Hamlet*, Act iv, Scene iii)

SECOND EDITION

Published by
THE INSTITUTE OF ECONOMIC AFFAIRS
1978

First published October 1976

Second Edition, revised and enlarged, February 1978

© THE INSTITUTE OF ECONOMIC AFFAIRS 1976, 1978

ISSN 0073-2818
ISBN 0-255 36105-X

Printed in Great Britain by
GORON PRO-PRINT CO LTD
6 Marlborough Road, Churchill Industrial Estate, Lancing, Sussex
Text set in 'Monotype' Baskerville

CONTENTS

[4]

[5]

[8]

PREFACE

The *Hobart Papers* are intended to contribute a stream of authoritative, independent and lucid analyses to understanding the application of economic thinking to private and governmental activity. Their characteristic concern has been the optimum use of scarce resources to satisfy consumer preferences and the extent to which it can be achieved in markets within the appropriate legal/institutional framework created by government or by other arrangements.

It has long been a common belief among economists since the classical thinkers of the 18th century that one of the most important functions of government was to create a monetary mechanism and to issue money.[1] The debates among economists have been on how far governments have performed this function efficiently and on the means of increasing or decreasing the power of government over the supply of money. But the general assumption has been that government had to control monetary policy and that each country had to have its own structure of monetary units.

This assumption is now questioned by Professor F. A. Hayek. He goes much more fully into the 'somewhat startling' departure from the classical assumption which he touched on in *Choice in Currency*, Occasional Paper No. 48, published in February 1976.

Even this short expansion of the theme indicates insights into the nature of money and its control for a wide range of readers: they should stimulate the student and suggest precepts for politicians. In effect, Professor Hayek is arguing that money is no different from other commodities and that it would be better supplied by competition between private issuers than by a monopoly of government. He argues, in the classic tradition of Adam Smith but with reference to the 20th century, that money is no exception to the rule that self-interest would be a better motive than benevolence in producing good results.

The advantages that Professor Hayek claims for competitive currencies are not only that they would remove the power of government to inflate the money supply but also that they would go a long way to prevent the destabilising fluctuations that government monopoly of money has precipitated over the last century of 'trade cycles' and, an urgent question in the

---

[1] In the Second Edition, Professor Hayek notes that it was not among those duties that Adam Smith said fell to the state (page 29).

1970s, make it more difficult for government to inflate its own expenditures.

Although the argument in places is necessarily abstract and requires close attention, the central theme is crystal clear: government has failed, must fail, and will continue to fail to supply good money. If government control of money is unavoidable Professor Hayek thinks a gold system better than any other; but he maintains that even gold would be found less dependable than competing paper currencies whose value would be maintained more or less stable because their issuers would have a strong inducement to limit their quantity or lose their business.

The argument for competitive currencies is in the direct line of descent in the thinking of the Austrian school of economists which Professor Lord Robbins largely introduced to Britain by bringing Professor Hayek to the London School of Economics in 1931. These two helped to make the works of Menger, Wieser, Böhm-Bawerk and Mises known to British students and teachers, but little further has been heard of the Austrian School until the last year or two. New interest in the Austrian School by economists in the USA is being followed by increasing attention in Britain, particularly by young economists. In this *Hobart Paper Special*, Professor Hayek refers to the writings of several of his predecessors and may further stimulate interest in the Austrian school of economics.

Although italicising is not common in IEA *Papers* it has been used here moderately to help especially readers new to economics to follow the steps in the argument.

Professor Hayek's *Hobart Special* comes at a time when, after pre-war monetary blunders said to have precipitated the 1929-32 Great Depression, nearly a third of a century of post-war 'monetary management' (or mis-management) by government, and when attempts at international management have hardly been more successful, economists are again looking to means of taking money out of the control of government altogether. In Hobart Paper 69 (*Gold or Paper?*) Professor E. Victor Morgan and Mrs Morgan re-examine the breakdown of monetary management since the war and re-assess the case for re-establishing a link between currency and gold. Some months ago Mr Peter Jay, the Economics Editor of *The Times*, proposed a Currency Commission.[1] Both of these approaches reflect the

[1] *The Times*, 15 April, 1976.

anxiety to reduce or remove the power of politicians over the supply of money and will seem to younger economists and to new generations in finance, commerce, industry and teaching to be radical departures from post-war economic thinking. Professor Hayek's proposal that the supply of money be put into the market-place along with other goods and services is even more revolutionary: he is arguing that the attempt for the past 50 years to depend on benevolence in government to manage money has failed and that the solution must lie in the self-interest of monetary agencies that will suffer by losing their livelihood if they do not supply currencies that users will find dependable and stable. Professor Hayek's *Hobart Special*, and the works of other economists who are trying to evolve methods of 'taking money out of politics', should stimulate economists and non-economists alike to re-examine the first principles of the control of money if civilised society is to continue.

The Institute is known for rapid publication—normally a few short weeks from completed MS to copy. Professor Hayek's movements from Austria to Scotland and then to London elongated the usual timetable of editing, processing for publication, and proof-reading. Even so these stages—for a manuscript twice the length of a typical Hobart—ran from early July to late September. I should like to thank Michael Solly, who excelled himself in helping to make this timetable possible, and Goron Pro-Print our printers, who worked rapidly and accurately.

Its constitution requires the Institute to dissociate its Trustees, Directors and Advisers from the argument and conclusion of its authors, but it presents this new short work by Professor Hayek as an important reconsideration of a classical precept from one of the world's leading thinkers.

August 1976   ARTHUR SELDON

PREFACE TO THE SECOND (EXTENDED) EDITION

For the Second (extended) Edition Professor Hayek has written many and sometimes lengthy additions to refine and amplify the argument. In all he has added about a third to two-fifths to the original text. (To identify the self-contained additions, both long and short, a single star is placed at the beginning and two stars at the end. There are in addition many other refinements of words, phrases and sentences, including numerous footnotes, *passim*.)

The *Hobart Paper* has now become a substantial text on the revolutionary proposal to replace state control of the money supply by competing private issuers in the market. When this principle was put to an august personage in the British banking system the urbane but complacent reply was 'That may be for the day after tomorrow'. This is a not uncommon reaction of practical men to the new thinking of academics. New ideas are liable to be dismissed as the work of theorists by hard-headed men who have to face the realities of everyday life. Practical men are so near their 'day-to-day problems' that they may see only the difficulties and obstacles and not the fundamental causes of error or failure. It is proper to reflect that the tree-feller cannot see the extent of the wood.

Even more fundamental change may sometimes have to be by radical reform rather than by piecemeal modification of a method or policy that has been shown to be defective. And the longer reform is delayed the more disturbing it may have to be. A man sinking in a bog cannot escape by a short step; his only hope may be a long leap.

The question is whether Professor Hayek's diagnosis—that state control of money has rarely supplied a dependable means of payment but has, in practice, been responsible for destabilising currencies and down the centuries for inflation—is correct or not. If it is correct, then tinkering with government monopoly control of money will not remove the defects and dangers.

This enlarged Second Edition should be earnestly studied not least by bankers, all the more when, as in Britain, they are not as removed from governmental—which means political—influence as they are in other countries. The additions will also make the Second Edition all the more valuable for teachers and students of economics who are more concerned with fundamental truths than with short-term expedients.

December 1977   A.S.

AUTHOR'S INTRODUCTION

For in every country of the world, I believe, the avarice and injustice of princes and sovereign states abusing the confidence of their subjects, have by degrees diminished the real quality of the metal, which had been originally contained in their coins.

ADAM SMITH
(*The Wealth of Nations* (1776), I. iv, Glasgow edn.,
Oxford, 1976, p. 43.)

In my despair about the hopelessness of finding a politically feasible solution to what is technically the simplest possible problem, namely to stop inflation, I threw out in a lecture delivered about a year ago[1] a somewhat startling suggestion, the further pursuit of which has opened quite unexpected new horizons. I could not resist pursuing the idea further, since the task of preventing inflation has always seemed to me to be of the greatest importance, not only because of the harm and suffering major inflations cause, but also because I have long been convinced that even mild inflations ultimately produce the recurring depressions and unemployment which have been a justified grievance against the free enterprise system and must be prevented if a free society is to survive.

The further pursuit of the suggestion that government should be deprived of its monopoly of the issue of money opened the most fascinating theoretical vistas and showed the possibility of arrangements which have never been considered. As soon as one succeeds in freeing oneself of the universally but tacitly accepted creed that a country must be supplied by its government with its own distinctive and exclusive currency, all sorts of interesting questions arise which have never been examined. The result was a foray into a wholly unexplored field. In this short work I can present no more than some discoveries made in the course of a first survey of the terrain. I am of course very much aware that I have only scratched the surface of the complex of new questions and that I am still very far from having solved all the problems which the existence of multiple concurrent currencies would raise. Indeed, I shall have to ask a number of questions to which I do not know the answer; nor can I discuss all the theoretical problems which the explanation of the new situation raises. Much more work will yet have to be

---

[1] See [31]. Numbers in square brackets will throughout refer to the Bibliography at the end of the *Paper* (pp. 134-140).

[13]

done on the subject; but there are already signs that the basic idea has stirred the imagination of others and that there are indeed some younger brains at work on the problem.[1]

The main result at this stage is that the chief blemish of the market order which has been the cause of well-justified reproaches, its susceptibility to recurrent periods of depression and unemployment, is a consequence of the age-old government monopoly of the issue of money. I have now no doubt whatever that private enterprise, if it had not been prevented by government, could and would long ago have provided the public with a choice of currencies, and those that prevailed in the competition would have been essentially stable in value and would have prevented both excessive stimulation of investment and the consequent periods of contraction.

The demand for the freedom of the issue of money will at first, with good reason, appear suspect to many, since in the past such demands have been raised again and again by a long series of cranks with strong inflationist inclinations. From most of the advocates of 'Free Banking' in the early 19th century (and even a substantial section of the advocates of the 'banking principle') to the agitators for a 'Free Money' (*Freigeld*)— Silvio Gesell [22] and the plans of Major C. H. Douglas [13], H. Rittershausen [51] and Henry Meulen [44]—in the 20th, they all agitated for free issue because they wanted *more* money. Often a suspicion that the government monopoly was inconsistent with the general principle of freedom of enterprise underlay their argument, but without exception they all believed that the monopoly had led to an undue restriction rather than to an excessive supply of money. They certainly did not recognise that government more often than any private enterprise had provided us with the *Schwundgeld* (shrinking money) that Silvio Gesell had recommended.

I will here merely add that, to keep to the main subject, I will not allow myself to be drawn into a discussion of the interesting methodological question of how it is possible to say something of significance about circumstances with which we have practically no experience, although this fact throws interesting light on the method of economic theory in general.

In conclusion I will merely say that this task has seemed to me important and urgent enough to interrupt for a few weeks the major undertaking to which all my efforts have been de-

[1] See [35], [59] and [60].

[14]

voted for the last few years and the completion of which still demands its concluding third volume.[1] The reader will, I hope, understand that in these circumstances, and against all my habits, after completing a first draft of the text of the present *Paper*, I left most of the exacting and time-consuming task of polishing the exposition and getting it ready for publication to the sympathetic endeavours of Mr Arthur Seldon, the Editorial Director of the Institute of Economic Affairs, whose beneficial care has already made much more readable some of my shorter essays published by that Institute, and who has been willing to assume this burden. His are in particular all the helpful headings of the sub-sections and the 'Questions for Discussion' at the end. And the much improved title of what I had intended to call *Concurrent Currencies* was suggested by the General Director of the Institute, Mr Ralph Harris. I am profoundly grateful to them for thus making possible the publication of this sketch. It would otherwise probably not have appeared for a long time, since I owe it to the readers of *Law, Legislation and Liberty* that I should not allow myself to be diverted from completing it by this rather special concern for longer than was necessary to get a somewhat rough outline of my argument on paper.

A special apology is due to those of my many friends to whom it will be obvious that, in the course of the last few years when I was occupied with wholly different problems, I have not read their publications closely related to the subject of this *Paper* which would probably have taught me much from which I could have profited in writing it.

Salzburg
30 June, 1976   F. A. HAYEK

---

[1] *Law, Legislation and Liberty:* Vol. I was *Rules and Order*, Routledge & Kegan Paul, 1973. Vol. 2, *The Mirage of Social Justice*, will appear about the same time as the present *Paper*. Vol. 3, *The Political Order of a Free Society*, nearing completion, will be published, I hope, in 1978.

A NOTE TO THE SECOND EDITION

It is just 13 months after I commenced writing this study and only a little more than six months since its first publication. It is therefore perhaps not very surprising that the additions I found desirable to make in this Second Edition are due more to further thinking about the questions raised than to any criticisms I have so far received. The comments so far, indeed, have expressed incredulous surprise more often than any objections to my argument.

Most of the additions therefore concern rather obvious points which perhaps I ought to have made more clearly in the First Edition. Only one of them, that on page 123 (page 98 of the First Edition) concerns a point on which further thought has led me to expect a somewhat different development from what I had suggested if the reform I propose were adopted. Indeed the clear distinction between two different kinds of competition, the first of which is likely to lead to the general acceptance of one widely used standard (or perhaps a very few such standards), while the second refers to the competition for the confidence of the public in the currency of a particular denomination, seems to me of ever greater importance. I have now sketched, in a somewhat longer insertion to Section XXIV (pp. 123-125), one of the most significant probable consequences, not originally foreseen by me.

I have made only minor stylistic changes to bring out more clearly what I meant to say. I have even let stand the difference between the more tentative tone at the beginning which, as will not have escaped the reader, gradually changes to a more confident tone as the argument proceeds. Further thought has so far only still more increased my confidence both in the desirability and the practicability of the fundamental change suggested.

Some important contributions to the problems considered here which were made at a Mont Pelerin Society conference held after the material for this Second Edition was prepared could not be used since I had immediately after to start on prolonged travels. I hope that particularly the papers presented then by W. Engels, D. L. Kemmerer, W. Stützel and R. Vaubel will soon be available in print. I have, however, inserted at a late stage a reply to a comment by Milton Friedman which seemed to me to demand a prompt response.

I should perhaps have added above to my reference to my preoccupation with other problems which have prevented me from giving the present argument all the attention which it deserves, that in fact my despair of ever again getting a tolerable money system under the present institutional structure is as much a result of the many years of study I have now devoted to the prevailing political order, and especially to the effects of government by a democratic assembly with unlimited powers, as to my earlier work when monetary theory was still one of my central interests.

I ought, perhaps, also to add, what I have often had occasion to explain but may never have stated in writing, that I strongly feel that the chief task of the economic theorist or political philosopher should be to operate on public opinion to make politically possible what today may be politically impossible, and that in consequence the objection that my proposals are at present impracticable does not in the least deter me from developing them.

Finally, after reading over once more the text of this Second Edition I feel I ought to tell the reader at the outset that in the field of money I do not want to prohibit government from doing anything except preventing others from doing things they might do better.

Freiburg im Breisgau   F. A. HAYEK

THE AUTHOR

FRIEDRICH AUGUST HAYEK, Dr Jur, Dr Sc Pol (Vienna), DSc (Econ.) (London), Visiting Professor at the University of Salzburg, Austria, 1970-74. Director of the Austrian Institute for Economic Research, 1927-31, and Lecturer in Economics at the University of Vienna, 1929-31. Tooke Professor of Economic Science and Statistics, University of London, 1931-50. Professor of Social and Moral Science, University of Chicago, 1950-62. Professor of Economics, University of Freiburg i.Brg., West Germany, 1962-68. He was awarded the Alfred Nobel Memorial Prize in Economic Sciences in 1974.

Professor Hayek's most important publications include *Prices and Production* (1931), *Monetary Theory and the Trade Cycle* (1933), *The Pure Theory of Capital* (1941), *The Road to Serfdom* (1944), *Individualism and Economic Order* (1948), *The Counter-Revolution of Science* (1952), and *The Constitution of Liberty* (1960). His latest works are a collection of his writings under the title *Studies in Philosophy, Politics and Economics* (1967) and *Law, Legislation and Liberty* (Vol. I: *Rules and Order*, 1973; Vol. II: *The Mirage of Social Justice*, 1976; Vol. III: *The Political Order of a Free Society* (forthcoming, 1978)). He has also edited several books and has published articles in the *Economic Journal*, *Economica* and other journals.

The IEA has published his *The Confusion of Language in Political Thought* (Occasional Paper 20, 1968), his Wincott Memorial Lecture, *Economic Freedom and Representative Government* (Occasional Paper 39, 1973), a collection of his writings with a new essay (assembled by Sudha Shenoy), *A Tiger by the Tail* (Hobart Paperback 4, 1972, Second Edition, 1978), an essay in *Verdict on Rent Control* (IEA Readings No. 7, 1972), *Full Employment at Any Price?* (Occasional Paper 45, 1975), and *Choice in Currency: A Way to Stop Inflation* (Occasional Paper 48, 1976).

I. THE PRACTICAL PROPOSAL

The concrete proposal for the near future, and the occasion for the examination of a much more far-reaching scheme, is that

the countries of the Common Market, preferably with the neutral countries of Europe (and possibly later the countries of North America) mutually bind themselves by formal treaty not to place any obstacles in the way of the free dealing throughout their territories in one another's currencies (including gold coins) or of a similar free exercise of the banking business by any institution legally established in any of their territories.

This would mean in the first instance the abolition of any kind of exchange control or regulation of the movement of money between these countries, as well as the full freedom to use any of the currencies for contracts and accounting. Further, it would mean the opportunity for any bank located in these countries to open branches in any other on the same terms as established banks.

Free trade in money

The purpose of this scheme is to impose upon existing monetary and financial agencies a very much needed discipline by making it impossible for any of them, or for any length of time, to issue a kind of money substantially less reliable and useful than the money of any other. As soon as the public became familiar with the new possibilities, any deviations from the straight path of providing an honest money would at once lead to the rapid displacement of the offending currency by others. And the individual countries, being deprived of the various dodges by which they are now able temporarily to conceal the effects of their actions by 'protecting' their currency, would be constrained to keep the value of their currencies tolerably stable.

Proposal more practicable than utopian European currency

This seems to me both preferable and more practicable than the utopian scheme of introducing a new European currency, which would ultimately only have the effect of more deeply entrenching the source and root of all monetary evil, the government monopoly of the issue and control of money. It would also seem that, if the countries were not prepared to adopt the more limited proposal advanced here, they would be even less willing to accept a common European currency. The idea of depriving government altogether of its age-old prerogative of monopolising money is still too unfamiliar and even alarming to most people to have any chance of being adopted in the near future. But people might learn to see the advantages if, at first at least, the currencies of the governments were allowed to compete for the favour of the public.

Though I strongly sympathise with the desire to complete the economic unification of Western Europe by completely freeing the flow of money between them, I have grave doubts about the desirability of doing so by creating a new European currency managed by any sort of supra-national authority. Quite apart from the extreme unlikelihood that the member countries would agree on the policy to be pursued in practice by a common monetary authority (and the practical inevitability of some countries getting a worse currency than they have now), it seems highly unlikely, even in the most favourable circumstances, that it would be administered better than the present national currencies. Moreover, in many respects a single international currency is not better but worse than a national currency if it is not better run. It would leave a country with a financially more sophisticated public not even the chance of escaping from the consequences of the crude prejudices governing the decisions of the others. The advantage of an international authority should be mainly to protect a member state from the harmful measures of others, not to force it to join in their follies.

Free trade in banking

The suggested extension of the free trade in money to free trade in banking is an absolutely essential part of the scheme if it is to achieve what is intended. First, bank deposits subject to cheque, and thus a sort of privately issued money, are today of course a part, and in most countries much the largest part, of the aggregate amount of generally accepted media of exchange. Secondly, the expansion and contraction of the separate national superstructures of bank credit are at present the chief excuse for national management of the basic money.

On the effects of the adoption of the proposal all I will add at this point is that it is of course intended to prevent national monetary and financial authorities from doing many things politically impossible to avoid so long as they have the power to do them. These are without exception harmful and against the long-run interest of the country doing them but politically inevitable as a temporary escape from acute difficulties. They include measures by which governments can most easily and quickly remove the causes of discontent of particular groups or sections but bound in the long run to disorganise and ultimately to destroy the market order.

Preventing government from concealing depreciation

The main advantage of the proposed scheme, in other words, is that it would prevent governments from 'protecting' the currencies they issue against the harmful consequences of their own measures, and therefore prevent them from further employing these harmful tools. They would become unable to conceal the depreciation of the money they issue, to prevent an outflow of money, capital, and other resources as a result of making their home use unfavourable, or to control prices—all measures which would, of course, tend to destroy the Common Market. The scheme would indeed seem to satisfy all the requirements of a common market better than a common currency without the need to establish a new international agency or to confer new powers on a supra-national authority.

The scheme would, to all intents and purposes, amount to a displacement of the national circulations only if the national monetary authorities misbehaved. Even then they could still ward off a complete displacement of the national currency by rapidly changing their ways. It is possible that in some very small countries with a good deal of international trade and tourism, the currency of one of the bigger countries might come to predominate, but, assuming a sensible policy, there is no reason why most of the existing currencies should not continue to be used for a long time. (It would, of course, be important that the parties did not enter into a tacit agreement not to supply so good a money that the citizens of the other nations would prefer it! And the presumption of guilt would of course always have to lie against the government whose money the public did not like!)

I do not think the scheme would prevent governments from doing anything they ought to do in the interest of a well-functioning economy, or which in the long run would benefit any substantial group. But this raises complex issues better discussed within the framework of the full development of the underlying principle.

II. THE GENERALISATION OF THE UNDERLYING PRINCIPLE

If the use of several concurrent currencies is to be seriously considered for immediate application in a limited area, it is evidently desirable to investigate the consequences of a general application of the principle on which this proposal is based. If we are to contemplate abolishing the exclusive use within each national territory of a single national currency issued by the government, and to admit on equal footing the currencies issued by other governments, the question at once arises whether it would not be equally desirable to do away altogether with the monopoly of government supplying money and to allow private enterprise to supply the public with other media of exchange it may prefer.

The questions this reform raises are at present much more theoretical than the practical proposal because the more far-reaching suggestion is clearly not only much too strange and alien to the general public to be considered for present application. The problems it raises are evidently also still much too little understood even by the experts for anyone to make a confident prediction about the precise consequences of such a scheme. Yet it is clearly possible that there is no necessity or even advantage in the now unquestioned and universally accepted government prerogative of producing money. It may indeed prove to be harmful and its abolition a great gain, opening the way for very beneficial developments. Discussion therefore cannot begin early enough. Though its realisation may be wholly impracticable so long as the public is mentally unprepared for it and uncritically accepts the dogma of the necessary government prerogative, this should no longer be allowed to act as a bar to the intellectual exploration of the fascinating theoretical problems the scheme raises.

Competition in currency not discussed by economists
It is an extraordinary truth that competing currencies have

[22]

until quite recently never been seriously examined.[1] There is no answer in the available literature to the question why a government monopoly of the provision of money is universally regarded as indispensable, or whether the belief is simply derived from the unexplained postulate that there must be within any given territory one single kind of money in circulation—which, so long as only gold and silver were seriously considered as possible kinds of money, might have appeared a definite convenience. Nor can we find an answer to the question of what would happen if that monopoly were abolished and the provision of money were thrown open to the competition of private concerns supplying different currencies. Most people seem to imagine that any proposal for private agencies to be allowed to issue money means that they should be allowed to issue the *same* money as anybody else (in token money this would, of course, simply amount to forgery) rather than *different* kinds of money clearly distinguishable by different denominations among which the public could choose freely.

Initial advantages of government monopoly in money

Perhaps when the money economy was only slowly spreading into the remoter regions, and one of the main problems was to teach large numbers the art of calculating in money (and that was not so very long ago), a single easily recognisable kind of money may have been of considerable assistance. And it may be argued that the exclusive use of such a single uniform sort of money greatly assisted comparison of prices and therefore the growth of competition and the market. Also, when the genuineness of metallic money could be ascertained only by a difficult process of assaying, for which the ordinary person had neither the skill nor the equipment, a strong case could be made for guaranteeing the fineness of the coins by the stamp of some generally recognised authority which, outside the great commercial centres, could be only the government. But today these initial advantages, which might have served as an excuse for governments to appropriate the exclusive right of issuing metallic money, certainly do not outweigh the

[1] But, though I had independently arrived at the realisation of the advantages possessed by independent competing currencies, I must now concede intellectual priority to Professor Benjamin Klein, who, in a paper written in 1970 and published in 1975 [35], until recently unknown to me, had clearly explained the chief advantage of competition among currencies.

disadvantages of this system. It has the defects of all monopolies: one must use their product even if it is unsatisfactory, and, above all, it prevents the discovery of better methods of satisfying a need for which a monopolist has no incentive. If the public understood what price in periodic inflation and instability it pays for the convenience of having to deal with only one kind of money in ordinary transactions, and not occasionally to have to contemplate the advantage of using other money than the familiar kind, it would probably find it very excessive. For this convenience is much less important than the opportunity to use a reliable money that will not periodically upset the smooth flow of the economy—an opportunity of which the public has been deprived by the government monopoly. But the people have never been given the opportunity to discover this advantage. Governments have at all times had a strong interest in persuading the public that the right to issue money belongs exclusively to them. And so long as, for all practical purposes, this meant the issue of gold, silver and copper coins, it did not matter so much as it does today, when we know that there are all kinds of other possible sorts of money, not least paper, which government is even less competent to handle and even more prone to abuse than metallic money.

III. THE ORIGIN OF THE GOVERNMENT PREROGATIVE OF MAKING MONEY

For more than 2,000 years the government prerogative or exclusive right of supplying money amounted in practice merely to the monopoly of minting coins of gold, silver or copper. It was during this period that this prerogative came to be accepted without question as an essential attribute of sovereignty—clothed with all the mystery which the sacred powers of the prince used to inspire. Perhaps this conception goes back to even before King Croesus of Lydia struck the first coins in the sixth century BC, to the time when it was usual merely to punch marks on the bars of metal to certify its fineness.

At any rate, the minting prerogative of the ruler was firmly established under the Roman emperors.[1] When, at the begin-

[1] W. Endemann [15], Vol. II, p. 171.

ning of the modern era, Jean Bodin developed the concept of sovereignty, he treated the right of coinage as one of the most important and essential parts of it.[1] The *regalia*, as these royal prerogatives were called in Latin, of which coinage, mining, and custom duties were the most important, were during the Middle Ages the chief sources of revenue of the princes and were viewed solely from this angle. It is evident that, as coinage spread, governments everywhere soon discovered that the exclusive right of coinage was a most important instrument of power as well as an attractive source of gain. From the beginning the prerogative was neither claimed nor conceded on the ground that it was for the general good but simply as an essential element of governmental power.[2] The coins served, indeed, largely as the symbols of might, like the flag, through which the ruler asserted his sovereignty, and told his people who their master was whose image the coins carried to the remotest parts of his realm.

Government certificate of metal weight and purity

The task the government was understood to assume was of course initially not so much to make money as to certify the weight and fineness of the materials that universally served as money,[3] which after the earliest times were only the three metals, gold, silver, and copper. It was supposed to be a task rather like that of establishing and certifying uniform weights and measures.

The pieces of metal were regarded as proper money only if

---

[1] J. Bodin [5], p. 176. Bodin, who understood more about money than most of his contemporaries, may well have hoped that the governments of large states would be more responsible than the thousands of minor princelings and cities who, during the later part of the Middle Ages, had acquired the minting privilege and sometimes abused it even more than the richer princes of large territories.

[2] The same applies to the postal monopoly which everywhere appears to provide a steadily deteriorating service and of which in Great Britain (according to *The Times*, 25 May, 1976) the General Secretary of the Union of Post Office Workers (!) said recently that 'Governments of both political complexions have reduced a once great public service to the level of a music-hall joke'. *Politically* the broadcasting monopoly may be even more dangerous, but *economically* I doubt whether any other monopoly has done as much damage as that of issuing money.

[3] Cf. Adam Smith [54, p. 40]: '... those public offices called mints: institutions exactly of the same nature with those of the aulnagers and stampmasters of woollen and linen cloth'.

they carried the stamp of the appropriate authority, whose duty was thought to be to assure that the coins had the proper weight and purity to give them their value.

During the Middle Ages, however, the superstition arose that it was the act of government that conferred the value upon the money. Although experience always proved otherwise, this doctrine of the *valor impositus*[1] was largely taken over by legal doctrine and served to some extent as justification of the constant vain attempts of the princes to impose the same value on coins containing a smaller amount of the precious metal. (In the early years of this century the medieval doctrine was revived by the German Professor G. F. Knapp; his *State Theory of Money* still seems to exercise some influence on contemporary legal theory.)[2]

There is no reason to doubt that private enterprise would, if permitted, have been capable of providing as good and at least as trustworthy coins. Indeed occasionally it did, or was commissioned by government to do so. Yet so long as the technical task of providing uniform and recognisable coins still presented major difficulties, it was at least a useful task which government performed. Unfortunately, governments soon discovered that it was not only useful but could also be made very profitable, at least so long as people had no alternative but to use the money they provided. The seignorage, the fee charged to cover the cost of minting, proved a very attractive source of revenue, and was soon increased far beyond the cost of manufacturing the coin. And from retaining an excessive part of the metal brought to the government mint to be struck into new coins, it was only a step to the practice, increasingly common during the Middle Ages, of recalling the circulating coins in order to recoin the various denominations with a lower gold or silver content. We shall consider the effect of these debasements in the next Section. But since the function of government in issuing money is no longer one of merely certifying the weight and fineness of a certain piece of metal, but involves a deliberate determination of the quantity of money to be issued, governments have become wholly inadequate for the task and, it can be said without qualifications, have incessantly and everywhere abused their trust to defraud the people.

[1] Endemann [15], p. 172.

[2] Knapp [36], and compare Mann [41].

The appearance of paper money

The government prerogative, which had originally referred only to the issue of coins because they were the only kind of money then used, was promptly extended to other kinds of money when they appeared on the scene. They arose originally when governments wanted money which they tried to raise by compulsory loans, for which they gave receipts that they ordered people to accept as money. The significance of the gradual appearance of government paper money, and soon of bank notes, is for our purposes complicated because for a long time the problem was not the appearance of new kinds of money with a different denomination, but the use as money of paper claims on the established kind of metallic money issued by government monopoly.

It is probably impossible for pieces of paper or other tokens of a material itself of no significant market value to come to be gradually accepted and held as money unless they represent a claim on some valuable object. To be accepted as money they must at first derive their value from another source, such as their convertibility into another kind of money. In consequence, gold and silver, or claims for them, remained for a long time the only kinds of money between which there could be any competition; and, since the sharp fall in its value in the 19th century, even silver ceased to be a serious competitor to gold. (The possibilities of bimetallism[1] are irrelevant for our present problems.)

Political and technical possibilities of controlling paper money

The position has become very different, however, since paper money established itself everywhere. The government monopoly of the issue of money was bad enough so long as metallic money predominated. But it became an unrelieved calamity since paper money (or other token money), which can provide the best and the worst money, came under political control. A money deliberately controlled in supply by an agency whose self-interest forced it to satisfy the wishes of the *users* might be the best. A money regulated to satisfy the demands of group interests is bound to be the worst possible (Section XVIII).

The value of paper money obviously can be regulated according to a variety of principles—even if it is more than

[1] Section VII, below, pp. 39-41.

doubtful that any democratic government with unlimited powers can ever manage it satisfactorily. Though historical experience would at first seem to justify the belief that only gold can provide a stable currency, and that all paper money is bound to depreciate sooner or later, all our insight into the processes determining the value of money tells us that this prejudice, though understandable, is unfounded. The *political* impossibility that governments will achieve it does not mean there is reason to doubt that it is *technically* possible to control the quantity of any kind of token money so that its value will behave in a desired manner, and that it will for this reason retain its acceptability and its value. It would therefore now be possible, if it were permitted, to have a variety of essentially different monies. They could represent not merely different quantities of the same metal, but also different abstract units fluctuating in their value relatively to one another. In the same way, we could have currencies circulating concurrently throughout many countries and offering the people a choice. This possibility appears, until recently, never to have been contemplated seriously. Even the most radical advocates of free enterprise, such as the philosopher Herbert Spencer[1] or the French economist Joseph Garnier,[2] seem to have advocated only private coinage, while the free banking movement of the mid-19th century agitated merely for the right to issue notes in terms of the standard currency.[3]

Monopoly of money has buttressed government power

While, as we shall see presently, government's exclusive right to issue and regulate money has certainly not helped to give us a better money than we would otherwise have had, and probably a very much worse one, it has of course become a chief instrument for prevailing governmental policies and profoundly assisted the general growth of governmental power. Much of contemporary politics is based on the assumption that government has the power to create and make people accept any amount of additional money it wishes. Governments will for this reason strongly defend their traditional rights. But for the same reason it is also most important that they should be taken from them.

A government ought not, any more than a private person, to

---

[1] Herbert Spencer [57]. [2] Joseph Garnier [21]. [3] Vera C. Smith [55].

be able (at least in peace-time) to take whatever it wants, but be limited strictly to the use of the means placed at its disposal by the representatives of the people, and to be unable to extend its resources beyond what the people have agreed to let it have. The modern expansion of government was largely assisted by the possibility of covering deficits by issuing money—usually on the pretence that it was thereby creating employment. It is perhaps significant, however, that Adam Smith [54, p. 687] does not mention the control of the issue of money among the 'only three duties [which] according to the system of natural liberty, the sovereign has to attend to'.

IV. THE PERSISTENT ABUSE OF THE GOVERNMENT PREROGATIVE

When one studies the history of money one cannot help wondering why people should have put up for so long with governments exercising an exclusive power over 2,000 years that was regularly used to exploit and defraud them. This can be explained only by the myth (that the government prerogative was necessary) becoming so firmly established that it did not occur even to the professional students of these matters (for a long time including the present writer[1]) ever to question it. But once the validity of the established doctrine is doubted its foundation is rapidly seen to be fragile.

We cannot trace the details of the nefarious activities of rulers in monopolising money beyond the time of the Greek philosopher Diogenes who is reported, as early as the fourth century BC, to have called money the politicians' game of dice. But from Roman times to the 17th century, when paper money in various forms begins to be significant, the history of coinage is an almost uninterrupted story of debasements or the continuous reduction of the metallic content of the coins and a corresponding increase in all commodity prices.

History is largely inflation engineered by government
Nobody has yet written a full history of these developments. It would indeed be all too monotonous and depressing a story,

[1] F. A. Hayek [29], pp. 324 *et seq.*

[29]

but I do not think it an exaggeration to say that history is largely a history of inflation, and usually of inflations engineered by governments and for the gain of governments—though the gold and silver discoveries in the 16th century had a similar effect. Historians have again and again attempted to justify inflation by claiming that it made possible the great periods of rapid economic progress. They have even produced a series of inflationist theories of history[1] which have, however, been clearly refuted by the evidence: prices in England and the United States were at the end of the period of their most rapid development almost exactly at the same level as two hundred years earlier. But their recurring rediscoverers are usually ignorant of the earlier discussions.

Early Middle Ages' deflation local or temporary

The early Middle Ages may have been a period of deflation that contributed to the economic decline of the whole of Europe. But even this is not certain. It would seem that on the whole the shrinking of trade led to the reduction of the amount of money in circulation, not the other way round. We find too many complaints about the dearness of commodities and the deterioration of the coin to accept deflation as more than a local phenomenon in regions where wars and migrations had destroyed the market and the money economy shrank as people buried their treasure. But where, as in Northern Italy, trade revived early, we find at once all the little princes vying with one another in diminishing the coin—a process which, in spite of some unsuccessful attempts of private merchants to provide a better medium of exchange, lasted throughout the following centuries until Italy came to be described as the country with the worst money and the best writers on money.

But though theologians and jurists joined in condemning these practices, they never ceased until the introduction of paper money provided governments with an even cheaper method of defrauding the people. Governments could not, of course, pursue the practices by which they forced bad money upon the people without the cruellest measures. As one legal treatise on the law of money sums up the history of punishment for merely refusing to accept the legal money:

[1] Especially Werner Sombart [56] and before him Archibald Alison [1] and others. Cf. on them Paul Barth [4], who has a whole chapter on 'History as a function of the value of money', and Marianne von Herzfeld [32].

'From Marco Polo we learn that, in the 13th century, Chinese law made the rejection of imperial paper money punishable by death, and twenty years in chains or, in some cases death, was the penalty provided for the refusal to accept French *assignats*. Early English law punished repudiation as *lese-majesty*. At the time of the American revolution, non-acceptance of Continental notes was treated as an enemy act and sometimes worked a forfeiture of the debt.'[1]

Absolutism suppressed merchants' attempts to create stable money

Some of the early foundations of banks at Amsterdam and elsewhere arose from attempts by merchants to secure for themselves a stable money, but rising absolutism soon suppressed all such efforts to create a non-governmental currency. Instead, it protected the rise of banks issuing notes in terms of the official government money. Even less than in the history of metallic money can we here sketch how this development opened the doors to new abuses of policy.

It is said that the Chinese had been driven by their experience with paper money to try to prohibit it for all time (of course unsuccessfully) before the Europeans ever invented it.[2] Certainly European governments, once they knew about this possibility, began to exploit it ruthlessly, not to provide people with good money, but to gain as much as possible from it for their revenue. Ever since the British Government in 1694 sold the Bank of England a limited monopoly of the issue of bank notes, the chief concern of governments has been not to let slip from their hands the power over money, formerly based on the prerogative of coinage, to really independent banks. For a time the ascendancy of the gold standard and the consequent belief that to maintain it was an important matter of prestige, and to be driven off it a national disgrace, put an effective restraint on this power. It gave the world the one long period—200 years or more—of relative stability during which modern industrialism could develop, albeit suffering from periodic crises. But as soon as it was widely understood some 50 years ago that the convertibility into gold was merely a method of controlling the *amount* of a currency, which was the real factor determining its

[1] A. Nussbaum [50], p. 53.

[2] On the Chinese events, see W. Vissering [61] and G. Tullock [58], who does not, however, allude to the often recounted story of the 'final prohibition'.

value, governments became only too anxious to escape that discipline, and money became more than ever before the plaything of politics. Only a few of the great powers preserved for a time tolerable monetary stability, and they brought it also to their colonial empires. But Eastern Europe and South America never knew a prolonged period of monetary stability.

But, while governments have never used their power to provide a decent money for any length of time, and have refrained from grossly abusing it only when they were under such a discipline as the gold standard imposed, the reason that should make us refuse any longer to tolerate this irresponsibility of government is that we know today that it is possible to control the quantity of a currency so as to prevent significant fluctuations in its purchasing power. Moreover, though there is every reason to mistrust government if not tied to the gold standard or the like, there is no reason to doubt that private enterprise whose business depended on succeeding in the attempt could keep stable the value of a money it issued.

Before we can proceed to show how such a system would work we must clear out of the way two prejudices that will probably give rise to unfounded objections against the proposal.

V. THE MYSTIQUE OF LEGAL TENDER

The first misconception concerns the concept of 'legal tender'. It is not of much significance for our purposes, but is widely believed to explain or justify government monopoly in the issue of money. The first shocked response to the proposal here discussed is usually 'But there must be a legal tender', as if this notion proved the necessity for a single government-issued money believed indispensable for the daily conduct of business.

In its strictly legal meaning, 'legal tender' signifies no more than a kind of money a creditor cannot refuse in discharge of a debt due to him in the money issued by government.[1] Even so, it is significant that the term has no authoritative definition

---

[1] Nussbaum [50], Mann [41] and Breckinridge [6].

in English statute law.[1] Elsewhere it simply refers to the means of discharging a debt contracted in terms of the money issued by government or due under an order of a court. In so far as government possesses the monopoly of issuing money and uses it to establish one kind of money, it must probably also have power to say by what kind of objects debts expressed in its currency can be discharged. But that means neither that all money need be legal tender, nor even that all objects given by the law the attribute of legal tender need to be money. (There are historical instances in which creditors have been compelled by courts to accept commodities such as tobacco, which could hardly be called money, in discharge of their claims for money.[2])

The superstition disproved by spontaneous money

The term 'legal tender' has, however, in popular imagination come to be surrounded by a penumbra of vague ideas about the supposed necessity for the state to provide money. This is a survival of the medieval idea that it is the state which somehow confers value on money it otherwise would not possess. And this, in turn, is true only to the very limited extent that government can force us to accept whatever it wishes in place of what we have contracted for; in this sense it can give the substitute the same value for the debtor as the original object of the contract. But the superstition that it is necessary for government (usually called the 'state' to make it sound better) to declare what is to be money, as if it had created the money which could not exist without it, probably originated in the naive belief that such a tool as money must have been 'invented' and given to us by some original inventor. This belief has been wholly displaced by our understanding of the spontaneous generation of such undesigned institutions by a process of social evolution of which money has since become the prime

[1] Mann [41], p. 38. On the other hand, the refusal until recently of English Courts to give judgement for paying in any other currency than the pound sterling has made this aspect of legal tender particularly influential in England. But this is likely to change after a recent decision (Miliangos v. George Frank Textiles Ltd [1975]) established that an English Court can give judgement in a foreign currency on a money claim in a foreign currency, so that, for instance, it is now possible in England to enforce a claim from a sale in Swiss francs. (*Financial Times*, 6 November, 1975: the report is reproduced in F. A. Hayek [31], pp. 45-6).

[2] Nussbaum [50], pp. 54-5.

paradigm (law, language and morals being the other main instances). When the medieval doctrine of the *valor impositus* was in this century revived by the much admired German Professor Knapp it prepared the way for a policy which in 1923 carried the German Mark down to $\dfrac{1}{1,000,000,000,000}$ of its former value!

Private money preferred

There certainly can be and has been money, even very satisfactory money, without government doing anything about it, though it has rarely been allowed to exist for long.[1] But a lesson is to be learned from the report of a Dutch author about China a hundred years ago who observed of the paper money then current in that part of the world that *'because it is not legal tender* and because it is no concern of the State it is generally accepted as money'.[2] We owe it to governments that within given national territories today in general only one kind of money is universally accepted. But whether this is desirable, or whether people could not, if they understood the advantage, get a much better kind of money without all the to-do about legal tender, is an open question. Moreover, a 'legal means of payment' (*gesetzliches Zahlungsmittel*) need not be specifically designated by a law. It is sufficient if the law enables the judge to decide in what sort of money a particular debt can be discharged.

The commonsense of the matter was put very clearly 80 years ago by a distinguished defender of a liberal economic policy, the lawyer, statistician and high civil servant Lord Farrer. In a paper written in 1895[3] he contended that if nations

'make nothing else but the standard unit [of value they have adopted] legal tender, there is no need and no room for

[1] Occasional attempts by the authorities of commercial cities to provide a money of at least a constant metallic content, such as the establishment of the Bank of Amsterdam, were for long periods fairly successful and their money used far beyond the national boundaries. But even in these cases the authorities sooner or later abused their quasi-monopoly positions. The Bank of Amsterdam was a state agency which people had to use for certain purposes and its money even as exclusive legal tender for payments above a certain amount. Nor was it available for ordinary small transactions or local business beyond the city limits. The same is roughly true of the similar experiments of Venice, Genoa, Hamburg and Nuremberg.

[2] Willem Vissering [61].

[3] Lord Farrer [17], p. 43.

[34]

the operation of any special law of legal tender. The ordinary law of contract does all that is necessary without any law giving special function to particular forms of currency. We have adopted a gold sovereign as our unit, or standard of value. If I promised to pay 100 sovereigns, it needs no special currency law of legal tender to say that I am bound to pay 100 sovereigns, and that, if required to pay the 100 sovereigns, I cannot discharge the obligation by anything else.'.

And he concludes, after examining typical applications of the legal tender conception, that

'*Looking to the above cases of the use or abuse of the law of legal tender other than the last* [i.e. that of subsidiary coins] *we see that they possess one character in common—viz. that the law in all of them enables a debtor to pay and requires a creditor to receive something different from that which their contract contemplated.* In fact it is a forced and unnatural construction put upon the dealings of men by arbitrary power'.[1]

To this he adds a few lines later that 'any Law of Legal Tender is in its own nature "suspect" '.[2]

Legal tender creates uncertainty

The truth is indeed that legal tender is simply a legal device to force people to accept in fulfilment of a contract something

---

[1] *Ibid.*, p. 45. The *locus classicus* on this subject from which I undoubtedly derived my views on it, though I had forgotten this when I wrote the First Edition of this *Paper*, is Carl Menger's discussion in 1892 [43a] of legal tender under the even more appropriate equivalent German term *Zwangskurs*. See pp. 98-106 of the reprint, especially p. 101, where the *Zwangskurs* is described as 'eine Massregel, die in der überwiegenden Zahl der Fälle den Zweck hat, gegen den Willen der Bevölkerung, zumindest durch einen Missbrauch der Münzhoheit oder des Notenregals entstandene pathologische (also exceptionelle[?]) Formen von Umlaufsmitteln, durch einen Missbrauch der Justizhoheit dem Verkehr aufzudrängen oder in demselben zu erhalten'; and p. 104 where Menger describes it as 'ein auf die Forderungsberechtigten geübter gesetzlicher Zwang, bei Summenschulden (bisweilen auch bei Schulden anderer Art) solche Geldsorten als Zahlung anzunehmen, welche dem ausdrücklich oder stillschweigend vereinbarten Inhalte der Forderungen nicht entsprechen, oder dieselben sich zu einem Wert aufdrangen zu lassen, der ihrem Wert im freien Verkehr nicht entspricht'. Especially interesting also is the first footnote on p. 102 in which Menger points out that there had been fairly general agreement on this among the liberal economists of the first half of the 19th century, while during the second half of that century, through the influence of the (presumably German) lawyers, the economists were led erroneously to regard legal tender as an attribute of perfect money.

[2] *Ibid.*, p. 47.

they never intended when they made the contract. It becomes thus, in certain circumstances, a factor that intensifies the uncertainty of dealings and consists, as Lord Farrer also remarked in the same context,

> 'in substituting for the free operation of voluntary contract, and a law which simply enforces the performance of such contracts, an artificial construction of contracts such as would never occur to the parties unless forced upon them by an arbitrary law'.

All this is well illustrated by the historical occasion when the expression 'legal tender' became widely known and treated as a definition of money. In the notorious 'legal tender cases', fought before the Supreme Court of the United States after the Civil War, the issue was whether creditors must accept at par current dollars in settlement of their claims for money they had lent when the dollar had a much higher value.[1] The same problem arose even more acutely at the end of the great European inflations after the First World War when, even in the extreme case of the German Mark, the principle 'Mark is Mark' was enforced until the end—although later some efforts were made to offer limited compensation to the worst sufferers.[2]

Taxes and contracts

A government must of course be free to determine in what currency taxes are to be paid and to make contracts in any currency it chooses (in this way it can support a currency it issues or wants to favour), but there is no reason why it should not accept other units of accounting as the basis of the assessment of taxes. In non-contractual payments such as damages or compensations for torts, the courts would have to decide the currency in which they have to be paid, and might for this purpose have to develop new rules; but there should be no need for special legislation.

[1] Cf. Nussbaum [50], pp. 586-592.

[2] In Austria after 1922 the name 'Schumpeter' had become almost a curse word among ordinary people, referring to the principle that 'Krone is Krone', because the economist J. A. Schumpeter, during his short tenure as Minister of Finance, had put his name to an order of council, merely spelling out what was undoubtedly valid law, namely that debts incurred in crowns when they had a higher value could be repaid in depreciated crowns, ultimately worth only a 15,000th part of their original value.

There is a real difficulty if a government-issued currency is replaced by another because the government has disappeared as a result of conquest, revolution, or the break-up of a nation. In that event the government taking over will usually make legal provisions about the treatment of private contracts expressed in terms of the vanished currency. If a private issuing bank ceased to operate and was unable to redeem its issue, this currency would presumably become valueless and the holders would have no enforceable claim for compensation. But the courts may decide that in such a case contracts between third parties in terms of that currency, concluded when there was reason to expect it to be stable, would have to be fulfilled in some other currency that came to the nearest presumed intention of the parties to the contract.

VI. THE CONFUSION ABOUT GRESHAM'S LAW

It is a misunderstanding of what is called Gresham's law to believe that the tendency for bad money to drive out good money makes a government monopoly necessary. The distinguished economist W. S. Jevons emphatically stated the law in the form that better money cannot drive out worse precisely to prove this. It is true he argued then against a proposal of the philosopher Herbert Spencer to throw the coinage of gold open to free competition, at a time when the only different currencies contemplated were coins of gold and silver. Perhaps Jevons, who had been led to economics by his experience as assayer at a mint, even more than his contemporaries in general, did not seriously contemplate the possibility of any other kind of currency. Nevertheless his indignation about what he described as Spencer's proposal

'that, as we trust the grocer to furnish us with pounds of tea, and the baker to send us loaves of bread, so we might trust Heaton and Sons, or some of the other enterprising firms of Birmingham, to supply us with sovereigns and shillings at their own risk and profit',[1]

[1] W. S. Jevons [34], p. 64, as against Herbert Spencer [57].

led him to the categorical declaration that generally, in his opinion, 'there is nothing less fit to be left to the action of competition than money'.[1]

It is perhaps characteristic that even Herbert Spencer had contemplated no more than that private enterprise should be allowed to produce the same sort of money as government then did, namely gold and silver coins. He appears to have thought them the only kind of money that could reasonably be contemplated, and in consequence that there would necessarily be fixed rates of exchange (namely of 1:1 if of the same weight and fineness) between the government and private money. In that event, indeed, Gresham's law would operate if any producer supplied shoddier ware. That this was in Jevons's mind is clear because he justified his condemnation of the proposal on the ground that

> 'while in all other matters everybody is led by self-interest to choose the better and reject the worse; but in the case of money, it would seem as if they paradoxically retain the worse and get rid of the better'.[2]

What Jevons, as so many others, seems to have overlooked, or regarded as irrelevant, is that Gresham's law will apply *only* to different kinds of money between which a fixed rate of exchange is enforced *by law*.[3] If the law makes two kinds of money perfect substitutes for the payment of debts and forces creditors to accept a coin of a smaller content of gold in the place of one with a larger content, debtors will, of course,

---

[1] Jevons, *ibid.*, p. 65. An earlier characteristic attempt to justify making banking and note issue an exception from a general advocacy of free competition is to be found in 1837 in the writings of S. J. Loyd (later Lord Overstone) [38], p.49: 'The ordinary advantages to the community arising from competition are that it tends to excite the ingenuity and exertion of the producers, and thus to secure to the public the best supply and quantity of the commodity at the lowest price, while all the evils arising from errors or miscalculations on the part of the producers will fall on themselves, and not on the public. With respect to a paper currency, however, the interest of the public is of a very different kind; a steady and equable regulation of its amount by fixed law is the end to be sought and the evil consequence of any error or miscalculation upon this point falls in a much greater proportion upon the public than upon the issuer.' It is obvious that Loyd thought only of the possibility of different agencies issuing the *same* currency, not of currencies of *different* denominations competing with one another.

[2] Jevons, *ibid.*, p. 82. Jevons's phrase is rather unfortunately chosen, because in the literal sense Gresham's law of course operates by people getting rid of the worse and retaining the better for other purposes.

[3] Cf. Hayek [30] and Fetter [17a].

pay only in the former and find a more profitable use for the substance of the latter.

With variable exchange rates, however, the inferior quality money would be valued at a lower rate and, particularly if it threatened to fall further in value, people would try to get rid of it as quickly as possible. The selection process would go on towards whatever they regarded as the best sort of money among those issued by the various agencies, and it would rapidly drive out money found inconvenient or worthless.[1] Indeed, whenever inflation got really rapid, all sorts of objects of a more stable value, from potatoes to cigarettes and bottles of brandy to eggs and foreign currencies like dollar bills, have come to be increasingly used as money,[2] so that at the end of the great German inflation it was contended that Gresham's law was false and the opposite true. It is not false, but it applies only if a *fixed rate of exchange* between the different forms of money is enforced.

VII. THE LIMITED EXPERIENCE WITH PARALLEL CURRENCIES AND TRADE COINS

So long as coins of the precious metals were the only practicable and generally acceptable kinds of money, with all close substitutes at least redeemable in them (copper having been reduced comparatively early to subsidiary token money), the only different kinds of money which appeared side by side were coins of gold and silver.

The multiplicity of coins with which the old money-changers had to deal consisted ultimately only of these two kinds, and their respective value within each group was determined by their content of either metal (which the expert but not the layman could ascertain). Most princes had tried to establish a fixed legal rate of exchange between gold and silver coins,

---

[1] If, as he is sometimes quoted, Gresham maintained that better money quite generally could not drive out worse, he was simply wrong, until we add his probably tacit presumption that a *fixed* rate of exchange was enforced.

[2] Cf. Bresciani-Turroni [7], p. 174: 'In monetary conditions characterised by a great distrust in the national currency, the principle of Gresham's law is reversed and *good money drives out bad*, and the value of the latter continually depreciates.' But even he does not point out that the critical difference is not the 'great distrust' but the presence or absence of effectively enforced fixed rates of exchange.

thereby creating what came to be called a bimetallic system. But since, in spite of very early suggestions that this rate be fixed by an international treaty,[1] governments established different exchange rates, each country tended to lose all the coins of the metal it under-valued relatively to the rates prevailing in other countries. The system was for that reason more correctly described as an alternative standard, the value of a currency depending on the metal which for the time being was over-valued. Shortly before it was finally abandoned in the second half of the 19th century, a last effort was made to establish internationally a uniform rate of exchange of 15½ between gold and silver. That attempt might have succeeded so long as there were no big changes in production. The comparatively large share of the total stocks of either metal that were in monetary use meant that, by an inflow or outflow into or from that use, their relative values could probably have been adjusted to the rate at which they were legally exchangeable as money.

Parallel currencies

In some countries, however, gold and silver had also been current for long periods side by side, their relative value fluctuating with changing conditions. This situation prevailed, for example, in England from 1663 to 1695 when, at last, by decreeing a rate of exchange between gold and silver coins at which gold was over-valued, England inadvertently established a gold standard.[2] The simultaneous circulation of coins of the two metals without a fixed rate of exchange between them was later called, by a scholar from Hanover where such a system existed until 1857, parallel currencies (*Parallelwährung*), to distinguish it from bimetallism.[3]

This is the only form in which parallel currencies were ever widely used, but it proved singularly inconvenient for a special reason. Since for most of the time gold was by weight more than 15 times as valuable as silver, it was evidently necessary to use the former for large and silver for the smaller (and copper for the still smaller) units. But, with variable values for the different kinds of coins, the smaller units were not constant

[1] In 1582 by G. Scaruffi [57].
[2] A. E. Feaveryear [16], p. 142.
[3] H. Grote [23].

fractions of the larger ones. In other words, the gold and the silver coins were parts of different systems without smaller or larger coins respectively of the same system being available.[1] This made any change from large to small units a problem, and nobody was able, even for his own purposes, to stick to one unit of account.

Except for a few instances in the Far East in recent times,[2] there seem to have been very few instances of concurrent circulation of currencies, and the memory of the parallel circulation of gold and silver coins has given the system rather a bad name. It is still interesting because it is the only important historical instance in which some of the problems arose that are generally raised by concurrent currencies. Not the least of them is that the concept of *the* quantity of money of a country or territory has strictly no meaning in such a system, since we can add the quantities of the different monies in circulation only after we know the relative value of the different units.

Trade coins

Nor are the somewhat different but more complex instances of the use of various trade coins[3] of much more help: the Maria Theresa Thaler in the regions around the Red Sea and the Mexican Dollar in the Far East, or the simultaneous circulation of two or more national currencies in some frontier districts or tourist centres. Indeed, our experience is so limited that we can do no better than fall back upon the usual procedure of classical economic theory and try to put together, from what we know from our common experience of the conduct of men in relevant situations, a sort of mental model (or thought experiment) of what is likely to happen if many men are exposed to new alternatives.

---

[1] For a time during the Middle Ages gold coins issued by the great commercial republics of Italy were used extensively in international trade and maintained over fairly long periods at a constant gold content, while at the same time the petty coins, mostly of silver, used in local retail trade suffered the regular fate of progressive debasement. (Cipolla [11], pp. 34 ff.)

[2] G. Tullock [58] and [59]; compare B. Klein [35].

[3] A convenient summary of information on trade coins is in Nussbaum [50], p. 315.

VIII. PUTTING PRIVATE TOKEN MONEY INTO CIRCULATION

I shall assume for the rest of this discussion that it will be possible to establish a number of institutions in various parts of the world which are free to issue notes in competition and similarly to carry cheque accounts in their individual denominations. I shall call these institutions simply 'banks', or 'issue banks' when necessary to distinguish them from other banks that do not choose to issue notes. I shall further assume that the name or denomination a bank chooses for its issue will be protected like a brand name or trade mark against unauthorised use, and that there will be the same protection against forgery as against that of any other document. These banks will then be vying for the use of their issue by the public by making them as convenient to use as possible.

The private Swiss 'ducat'

Since readers will probably at once ask how such issues can come to be generally accepted as money, the best way to begin is probably to describe how I would proceed if I were in charge of, say, one of the major Swiss joint stock banks. Assuming it to be legally possible (which I have not examined), I would announce the issue of non-interest bearing certificates or notes, and the readiness to open current cheque accounts, in terms of a unit with a distinct registered trade name such as 'ducat'. The only legal obligation I would assume would be to redeem these notes and deposits on demand with, at the option of the holder, either 5 Swiss francs or 5 D-marks or 2 dollars per ducat. This redemption value would however be intended only as a floor below which the value of the unit could not fall because I would announce at the same time my intention to regulate the quantity of the ducats so as to keep their (precisely defined) purchasing power as nearly as possible constant. I would also explain to the public that I was fully aware I could hope to keep these ducats in circulation only if I fulfilled the expectation that their real value would be kept approximately constant. And I would announce that I proposed from time to time to state the precise commodity equivalent in terms of which I intended to keep the value of the ducat constant, but that I reserved the right, after announcement, to alter the composition of the commodity standard as experience and the revealed preferences of the public suggested.

*

It would, however, clearly be necessary that, though it seems neither necessary nor desirable that the issuing bank legally commits itself to maintain the value of its unit, it should in its loan contracts specify that any loan could be repaid either at the nominal figure in its own currency, or by corresponding amounts of any other currency or currencies sufficient to buy in the market the commodity equivalent which at the time of making the loan it had used as its standard. Since the bank would have to issue its currency largely through lending, intending borrowers might well be deterred by the formal possibility of the bank arbitrarily raising the value of its currency, that they may well have to be explicitly reassured against such a possibility. **1

These certificates or notes, and the equivalent book credits, would be made available to the public by short-term loans or sale against other currencies. The units would presumably, because of the option they offered, sell from the outset at a premium above the value of any one of the currencies in which they were redeemable. And, as these governmental currencies continued to depreciate in real terms, this premium would increase. The real value at the price at which the ducats were first sold would serve as the standard the issuer would have to try to keep constant. If the existing currencies continued to depreciate (and the availability of a stable alternative might indeed accelerate the process) the demand for the stable currency would rapidly increase and competing enterprises offering similar but differently-named units would soon emerge.

The sale (over the counter or by auction) would initially be the chief form of issue of the new currency. After a regular market had established itself, it would normally be issued only in the course of ordinary banking business, i.e. through short-term loans.

Constant but not fixed value
It might be expedient that the issuing institution should from the outset announce precisely the collection of commodities in terms of which it would aim to keep the value of the 'ducat'

---

1 [To assist readers of the First Edition to identify major additions, we have inserted a single asterisk at the beginning and double asterisks at the end of substantial, self-contained new passages. – ED.]

constant. But it would be neither necessary nor desirable that it tie itself legally to a particular standard. Experience of the response of the public to competing offers would gradually show which combination of commodities constituted the most desired standard at any time and place. Changes in the importance of the commodities, the volume in which they were traded, and the relative stability or sensitivity of their prices (especially the degree to which they were determined competitively or not) might suggest alterations to make the currency more popular. On the whole I would expect that, for reasons to be explained later (Section XIII), a collection of raw material prices, such as has been suggested as the basis of a commodity reserve standard,[1] would seem most appropriate, both from the point of view of the issuing bank and from that of the effects of the stability of the economic process as a whole.

Control of value by competition

In most respects, indeed, the proposed system should prove a more practicable method of achieving all that was hoped from a commodity reserve standard or some other form of 'tabular standard.' At the same time it would remove the necessity of making it fully automatic by taking the control from a monopolistic authority and entrusting it to private concerns. The threat of the speedy loss of their whole business if they failed to meet expectations (and how any government organisation would be certain to abuse the opportunity to play with raw material prices!) would provide a much stronger safeguard than any that could be devised against a government monopoly. Competition would certainly prove a more effective constraint, forcing the issuing institutions to keep the value of their currency constant (in terms of a stated collection of commodities), than would any obligation to redeem the currency in those commodities (or in gold). And it would be an infinitely cheaper method than the accumulation and the storing of valuable materials.

The kind of trust on which private money would rest would not be very different from the trust on which today all private banking rests (or in the United States rested before the governmental deposit insurance scheme!). People today trust that a bank, to preserve its business, will arrange its affairs so that it

[1] Cf. Hayek [30], pp. 318-320.

will at all times be able to exchange demand deposits for cash, although they know that banks do not have enough cash to do so if everyone exercised his right to demand instant payment at the same time. Similarly, under the proposed scheme, the managers of the bank would learn that its business depended on the unshaken confidence that it would continue to regulate its issue of ducats (etc.) so that their purchasing power remained approximately constant.

Is the risk in the venture therefore too big to justify entry by men with the kind of conservative temper its successful conduct probably requires?[1] It is not to be denied that, once announced and undertaken, the decision on how large the commitment was to grow would be taken out of the hands of the issuing institution. To achieve its announced aim of maintaining the purchasing power of its currency constant, the amount would have to be promptly adapted to any change of demand, whether increase or decrease. Indeed, so long as the bank succeeded in keeping the value of its currency constant, there would be little reason to fear a sudden large reduction of the demand for it (though successful competitors might well make considerable inroads on its circulation). The most embarrassing development might be a rapid growth of demand beyond the limits a private institution likes to handle. But we can be fairly sure that, in the event of such success, new competition would soon relieve a bank of this anxiety.

The issuing bank could, at first, at no prohibitive cost keep in cash a 100 per cent reserve of the currencies in terms of which it had undertaken to redeem its issue and still treat the premiums received as freely available for general business. But once these other currencies had, as the result of further

---

[1] On the question of its attractiveness the discussion by S. Fischer [18] of the notorious reluctance of enterprise to issue indexed bonds is somewhat relevant. It is true that a gradual increase of the value of the notes issued by a bank in terms of other concurrent currencies might produce a situation in which the aggregate value of its outstanding notes (*plus* its liabilities from other sources) would exceed its assets. The bank would of course not be legally liable to redeem its notes at this value, but it could preserve this business only if it did in fact promptly buy at the current rate any of its notes offered to it. So long as it succeeded in maintaining the real value of its notes, it would never be called upon to buy back more than a fraction of the outstanding circulation. Probably no one would doubt that an art dealer who owns the plates of the engravings of a famous artist could, so long as his works remained in fashion, maintain the market value of these engravings by judiciously selling and buying, even though he could never buy up all the existing prints. Similarly, a bank could certainly maintain the value of its notes even though it could never buy back all the outstanding ones.

inflation, substantially depreciated relative to the ducat, the bank would have to be prepared, in order to maintain the value of the ducat, to buy back substantial amounts of ducats at the prevailing higher rate of exchange. This means that it would have to be able rapidly to liquidate investments of very large amounts indeed. These investments would therefore have to be chosen very carefully if a temporary rush of demand for its currency were not to lead to later embarrassment when the institution that had initiated the development had to share the market with imitators. Incidentally, the difficulty of finding investments of an assured stable value to match similar obligations would not be anything like as difficult for such a bank as we are considering as present-day bankers seem to find it: all the loans made in its own currency would of course represent such stable assets. The curious fact that such an issuing bank would have claims and obligations in terms of a unit the value of which it determined itself, though it could not do so arbitrarily or capriciously without destroying the basis of its business, may at first appear disturbing but should not create real difficulties. What may at first appear somewhat puzzling accounting problems largely disappear when it is remembered that such a bank would of course keep its accounts in terms of its own currency. The outstanding notes and deposits of such a bank are not claims on it in terms of some other unit of value; it determines itself the value of the unit in terms of which it has debts and claims and keeps its books. This will cease to seem shocking when we remember that this is precisely what practically all central banks have been doing for nearly half a century—their notes were of course redeemable in precisely nothing. But notes which may appreciate relatively to most other capital assets may indeed present to accountants problems with which they never before had to deal. Initially the issuing bank would of course be under a legal obligation to redeem its currency in terms of the other currencies against which it was at first issued. But after it has existed for some time their value may have shrunk to very little or they may have altogether disappeared.[1]

---

[1] A real difficulty could arise if a sudden large increase in the demand for such a stable currency, perhaps due to some acute economic crisis, had to be met by selling large amounts of it against other currencies. The bank would of course have to prevent such a rise in the value and could do so only by increasing its supply. But selling against other currencies would give it assets likely to depreciate

[Contd. on page 47]

IX. COMPETITION BETWEEN BANKS ISSUING DIFFERENT CURRENCIES

It has for so long been treated as a self-evident proposition that the supply of money cannot be left to competition that probably few people could explain why. As we have seen, the explanation appears to be that it has always been assumed that there must be only *one* uniform kind of currency in a country, and that competition meant that its amount was to be determined by several agencies issuing it independently. It is, however, clearly not practicable to allow tokens with the same name and readily exchangeable against each other to be issued competitively, since nobody would be in a position to control their quantity and therefore be responsible for their value. The question we have to consider is whether competition between the issuers of clearly distinguishable kinds of currency consisting of *different* units would not give us a better kind of money than we have ever had, far outweighing the inconvenience of encountering (but for most people not even having to handle) more than one kind.

In this condition the value of the currency issued by one bank would not necessarily be affected by the supplies of other currencies by different institutions (private or governmental). And it should be in the power of each issuer of a distinct currency to regulate its quantity so as to make it most acceptable to the public—and competition would force him to do so. Indeed, he would know that the penalty for failing to fulfil the expectations raised would be the prompt loss of the business. Successful entry into it would evidently be a very profitable venture, and success would depend on establishing the credibility and trust that the bank was able and determined to carry out its declared intentions. It would seem that in this situation sheer desire for gain would produce a better money than government has ever produced.[1]

[*Contd. from page 46*]
in terms of its own currency. It probably could not increase its short-term lending very rapidly, even if it offered to lend at a very low rate of interest—even though in such a situation it would be safer to lend even at a small negative rate of interest than to sell against other currencies. And it would probably be possible to grant long-term loans at very low rates of interest against negotiable securities (in terms of its own currency) which it should be easy to sell if the sudden increase of demand for its currency should be as rapidly reversed.

[1] Apart from notes and cheque deposits in its distinctive currency, an issuing bank would clearly also have to provide fractional coins; and the availability of

Effects of competition

It seems to me to be fairly certain that

(a) *a money generally expected to preserve its purchasing power approximately constant would be in continuous demand so long as the people were free to use it;*

(b) *with such a continuing demand depending on success in keeping the value of the currency constant one could trust the issuing banks to make every effort to achieve this better than would any monopolist who runs no risk by depreciating his money;*

(c) *the issuing institution could achieve this result by regulating the quantity of its issue;* and

(d) *such a regulation of the quantity of each currency would constitute the best of all practicable methods of regulating the quantity of media of exchange for all possible purposes.*

Clearly a number of competing issuers of different currencies would have to compete in the quality of the currencies they offered for loan or sale. Once the competing issuers had credibly demonstrated that they provided currencies more suitable to the needs of the public than government has ever provided, there would be no obstacle to their becoming generally accepted in preference to the governmental cur-

[*Contd. from page 47*]
convenient fractional coins in that currency might well be an important factor in making it popular. It would also probably be the habitual use of one sort of fractional coins (especially in slot machines, fares, tips, etc.) which would secure the predominance of one currency in the retail trade of one locality. The effective competition between different currencies would probably be largely confined to inter-business use, with retail trade following the decisions about the currency in which wages and salaries were to be paid.

Certain special problems would arise where present sales practices are based on the general use of uniform coins of a few relatively small standard units, as, e.g., in vending machines, transportation or telephones. Probably even in localities in which several different currencies were in general use, one set of small coins would come to dominate. If, as seems probable, most of these competing currencies were kept at practically the same value, the technical problem of the use of coins might be solved in any one of various ways. One might be that one institution, e.g. an association of retailers, specialised in the issue of uniform coins at slightly fluctuating market prices. Tradesmen and transport and communication undertakings of a locality might join to sell, at market prices and probably through the banks, a common set of tokens for all automats in the locality. We can certainly expect commercial inventiveness rapidly to solve such minor difficulties. Another possible development would be the replacement of the present coins by plastic or similar tokens with electronic markings which every cash register and slot machine would be able to sort out, and the 'signature' of which would be legally protected against forgery as any other document of value.

rencies—at least in countries in which government had removed all obstacles to their use. The appearance and increasing use of the new currencies would, of course, decrease the demand for the existing national ones and, unless their volume was rapidly reduced, would lead to their depreciation. This is the process by which the unreliable currencies would gradually all be eliminated. The condition required in order that this displacement of the government money should terminate before it had entirely disappeared would be that government reformed and saw to it that the issue of its currency was regulated on the same principles as those of the competing private institutions. It is not very likely that it would succeed, because to prevent an accelerating depreciation of its currency it would have to respond to the new currencies by a rapid contraction of its own issue.

'A thousand hounds': the vigilant press

The competition between the issuing banks would be made very acute by the close scrutiny of their conduct by the press and at the currency exchange. For a decision so important for business as which currency to use in contracts and accounts, all possible information would be supplied daily in the financial press, and have to be provided by the issuing banks themselves for the information of the public. Indeed, a thousand hounds would be after the unfortunate banker who failed in the prompt responses required to ensure the safeguarding of the value of the currency he issues. The papers would probably print a

TABLE I

ILLUSTRATION OF POSSIBLE CURRENCY PRICE DEVIATIONS

Currency	Deviation from	
	Announced Standard %	Our Test Standard %
Ducats (SGB)	−0·04	−0·04
Florins (FNB)	+0·02	+0·03
Mengers (WK)	+0·10	+0·10
Piasters (DBS)	−0·06	−0·12
Reals (CNB)	**−1·02**	**−1·01**
Shekels (ORT)	−0·45	−0·45
Talents (ATBC)	+0·26	+0·02

table daily, not only of the current rates of exchange between the currencies but also of the current value, and the deviation of each of the currencies likely to be used by their readers from the announced standard of value in terms of commodities. These tables might look something like Table I (with the initials of the issuing institution given after the name of the currency it issues).

Nothing would be more feared by the bankers than to see the quotation of their currency in heavy type to indicate that the real value had fallen below the standard of tolerance set by the paper publishing the table.

Three questions

This sketch of the competition between several private issuing institutions presupposes answers to a number of questions we shall have to examine in more detail in succeeding sections.

—The first is whether a competing institution issuing its distinctive currency will always be able to regulate its value by controlling its quantity so as to make it more attractive to people than other currencies, and how far other issuers of currencies can by their policy interfere with these efforts.

—The second is which value (or other attribute of a currency) the public will prefer if different banks announce that it is their intention (and demonstrate their ability) to keep announced values of their currency constant.

—A third and no less important question is whether the kind of money most people will individually prefer to use will also best serve the aims of all. Though one might at first think that this must necessarily be so, it is not inevitably true. It is conceivable that the success of people's efforts will depend not only on the money they themselves use but also on the effects of the money others use, and the benefits they derive for themselves from using a particular kind of money may conceivably be more than offset by the disturbances caused by its general use. I do not believe this to be the case in the present instance, but the question certainly requires explicit consideration.

Before we can discuss further the interaction between currencies it will be expedient to devote a section to precisely what we mean by money or currency and its different kinds, and the various ways in which they may differ from one another.

X. A DIGRESSION ON THE DEFINITION OF MONEY

Money is usually defined as *the* generally acceptable medium of exchange,[1] but there is no reason why within a given community there should be only one kind of money that is generally (or at least widely) accepted. In the Austrian border town in which I have been living for the past few years, shopkeepers and most other business people will usually accept D-Marks as readily as Austrian schillings, and only the law prevents German banks in Salzburg from doing their business in D-Marks in the same manner as they do 10 miles away on the German side of the border. The same is true of hundreds of other tourist centres in Austria frequented mainly by Germans. In most of them dollars will also be accepted nearly as readily as D-Marks. I believe the situation is not very different on both sides of long stretches of the border between the United States and Canada or Mexico, and probably along many other frontiers.

But though in such regions everybody may be ready to accept several currencies at the current rate of exchange, individuals may use different kinds of money to hold (as liquidity reserves), to make contracts for deferred payments, or to keep their accounts in, and the community may respond in the same manner to changes in the amounts of the different currencies.

By referring to different kinds of money we have in mind units of different denomination whose relative values may

---

[1] This definition was established by Carl Menger [43], whose work also ought to have finally disposed of the medieval conception that money, or the value of money, was a creation of the state. Vissering [61], p. 9, reports that in early times the Chinese expressed their notions of money by a term meaning literally 'current merchandise'. The now more widely used expression that money is the most liquid asset comes, of course (as Carlile [8] pointed out as early as 1901), to the same thing. To serve as a widely accepted medium of exchange is the only function which an object must perform to qualify as money, though a generally accepted medium of exchange will generally acquire also the further functions of unit of account, store of value, standard of deferred payment, etc. The definition of money as 'means of payment' is, however, purely circular, since this concept presupposed debts incurred in terms of money. Cf. L. v. Mises [45], pp. 34 ff.

The definition of money as the generally acceptable medium of exchange does not, of course, necessarily mean that even within one national territory there must be a single kind of money which is more acceptable than all others; there may be several equally acceptable kinds of money (which we may more conveniently call currencies), particularly if one kind can be quickly exchanged into the others at a known, though not fixed, rate.

fluctuate against one another. These fluctuating values must be emphasised because they are not the only way in which media of exchange may differ from one another. They may also, even when expressed in terms of the same unit, differ widely in their degree of acceptability (or liquidity, i.e. in the very quality which makes them money), or the groups of people that readily accept them. This means that different kinds of money can differ from one another in more than one dimension.

No clear distinction between money and non-money

It also means that, although we usually assume there is a sharp line of distinction between what is money and what is not—and the law generally tries to make such a distinction—so far as the causal effects of monetary events are concerned, there is no such clear difference. What we find is rather a continuum in which objects of various degrees of liquidity, or with values which can fluctuate independently of each other, shade into each other in the degree to which they function as money.[1]

I have always found it useful to explain to students that it has been rather a misfortune that we describe money by a noun, and that it would be more helpful for the explanation of monetary phenomena if 'money' were an adjective describing a property which different things could possess to varying *degrees*.[2] 'Currency' is, for this reason, more appropriate, since objects can 'have currency' to varying degrees and through different regions or sectors of the population.

Pseudo-exactness, statistical measurement, and scientific truth

Here we encounter a difficulty we frequently meet in our efforts to explain the ill-defined phenomena of economic life. In order to simplify our exposition of what are very complex interconnections that otherwise would become difficult to follow, we introduce sharp distinctions where in real life different attributes of the objects shade into each other. A similar situation arises where we try to draw sharp distinctions between such objects as commodities and services, consumers'

[1] Cf. J. R. Hicks [33].

[2] Machlup for this reason speaks occasionally, e.g. [39], p. 225, of 'moneyness' and 'near-moneyness'.

[52]

goods and capital goods, durable and perishable, reproducible and non-reproducible, specific and versatile, or substitutable and non-substitutable goods. All are very important distinctions but they can become very misleading if, in the popular striving for pseudo-exactness, we treat these classes as measurable quantities. This involves a simplification which is perhaps sometimes necessary but always dangerous and has led to many errors in economics. Though the differences are significant, this does not mean we can neatly and unambiguously divide these things into two, or any other number of, distinct classes. We often do, and perhaps often must talk as if this division were true, but the usage can be very deceptive and produce wholly erroneous conclusions.[1]

Legal fictions and defective economic theory

Similarly, the legal fiction that there is one clearly defined thing called 'money' that can be sharply distinguished from other things, a fiction introduced to satisfy the work of the lawyer or judge, was never true so far as things are to be referred to which have the characteristic effects of events on the side of money. Yet it has done much harm through leading to the demand that, for certain purposes, only 'money' issued by government may be used, or that there must always be some single kind of object which can be referred to as *the* 'money' of the country. It has also, as we shall see, led to the development in economic theory of an explanation of the value of units of money which, though under its simplified assumptions it gives some useful approximations, is of no help for the kind of problems we have to examine here.

For what follows it will be important to keep in mind that different kinds of money can differ from one another in two distinct although not wholly unrelated dimensions: acceptability (or liquidity) and the expected behaviour (stability or variability) of its value. The expectation of stability will evi-

---

[1] It is a practice particularly congenial to statisticians, the applicability of whose techniques frequently depends on using it. Though the popular tendency in economics to accept only *statistically* testable theories has given us some useful gross approximations to the truth, such as the quantity theory of the value of money, they have acquired a quite undeserved reputation. The idea discussed in the text makes most quantitative formulations of economic theory inadequate in practice. To introduce sharp distinctions which do not exist in the real world in order to make a subject susceptible to mathematical treatment is not to make it more scientific but rather less so.

dently affect the liquidity of a particular kind of money, but it may be that in the short run liquidity may sometimes be more important than stability, or that the acceptability of a more stable money may for some reason be confined to rather limited circles.

Meanings and definitions

This is perhaps the most convenient place to add explicit statements concerning the meanings in which we shall use other frequently recurring terms. It will have become clear that in the present connection it is rather more expedient to speak of 'currencies' than 'monies', not only because it is easier to use the former term in the plural but also because, as we have seen, 'currency' emphasises a certain attribute. We shall also use 'currency', perhaps somewhat in conflict with the original meaning of the term, to include not only pieces of paper and other sorts of 'hand-to-hand money', but also bank balances subject to cheque and other media of exchange that can be used for most of the purposes for which cheques are used. There is, however, as we have just pointed out, no need for a very sharp distinction between what is and what is not money. The reader will do best if he remains aware that we have to deal with a *range* of objects of varying degrees of acceptability which imperceptibly shade at the lower end into objects that are clearly not money.

Although we shall frequently refer to the agencies issuing currency simply as 'banks', this is not meant to imply that all banks will be issuing money. The term 'rate of exchange' will be used throughout for rates of exchange between currencies, and the term 'currency exchange' (analogous to stock exchange) for the organised currency market. Occasionally we shall also speak of 'money substitutes' when we have to consider border-line cases in the scale of liquidity—such as travellers' cheques, credit cards, and overdrafts—where it would be quite arbitrary to assert that they either are or are not part of the circulation of currency.

XI. THE POSSIBILITY OF CONTROLLING THE VALUE OF A COMPETITIVE CURRENCY

The chief attraction the issuer of a competitive currency has to offer to his customers is the assurance that its value will be kept stable (or otherwise be made to behave in a predictable manner). We shall leave for Section XII the question of precisely what kind of stability the public will probably prefer. For the moment we shall concentrate on whether an issuing bank in competition with other issuers of similar currencies will have the power to control the quantity of its distinctive issue so as to determine the value it will command in the market.

The expected value of a currency will, of course, not be the only consideration that will lead the public to borrow or buy it. But the expected value will be the decisive factor determining how much of it the public will wish to hold, and the issuing bank will soon discover that the desire of the public to *hold* its currency will be the essential circumstance on which its value depends. At first it might perhaps seem obvious that the exclusive issuer of a currency, who as such has complete control over its supply, will be able to determine its price so long as there is anyone who wants it at that price. If, as we shall provisionally assume, the aim of the issuing bank is to keep constant the aggregate price in terms of its currency of a particular collection of commodities it would, by regulating the amount of the currency in circulation, have to counteract any tendency of that aggregate price to rise or fall.

Control by selling/buying currency and (short-term) lending
The issuing bank will have two methods of altering the volume of its currency in circulation: it can sell or buy its currency against other currencies (or securities and possibly some commodities); and it can contract or expand its lending activities. In order to retain control over its outstanding circulation, it will on the whole have to confine its lending to relatively short-time contracts so that, by reducing or temporarily stopping new lending, current repayments of outstanding loans would bring about a rapid reduction of its total issue.

To assure the constancy of the value of its currency the main consideration would have to be never to increase it beyond the total the public is prepared to hold without increasing expenditure in it so as to drive up prices of commodities in terms of it;

it must also never reduce its supply below the total the public is prepared to hold without reducing expenditure in it and driving prices down. In practice, many or even most of the commodities in terms of which the currency is to be kept stable would be currently traded and quoted chiefly in terms of some other competing currencies (especially if, as we suggest in Section XIII, it will be mainly prices of raw materials or wholesale prices of foodstuffs). The bank would therefore have to look to the effect of changes in its circulation, not so much directly on the prices of other *commodities*, but on the rates of exchange with the *currencies* against which they are chiefly traded. Though the task of ascertaining the appropriate rates of exchange (considering the given rates of exchange between the different currencies) would be complex, computers would help with almost instantaneous calculation, so the bank would know hour by hour whether to increase or decrease the amounts of its currency to be offered as loans or for sale. Quick and immediate action would have to be taken by buying or selling on the currency exchange, but a lasting effect would be achieved only by altering the lending policy.

*

Current issuing policy

Perhaps I ought to spell out here in more detail how an issuing bank would have to proceed in order to keep the chosen value of its currency constant. The basis of the daily decisions on its lending policy (and its sales and purchases of currencies on the currency exchange) would have to be the result of a constant calculation provided by a computer into which the latest information about commodity prices and rates of exchange would be constantly fed as it arrived. The character of this calculation can be illustrated by the following abridged table (Table II). (I am neglecting here the question how far the costs of transport from the chief market to some common centre, or perhaps separate items representing the costs of different forms of transport, should be considered or not.)

The essential information would be the guide number at the lower right-hand corner, resulting either from the quantities of the different commodities being so chosen that at the base date their aggregate price in Ducats was 1,000, or 1,000 was used as the base of an index number. This figure and its current changes would serve as a signal telling all executive officers of the bank what to do. A 1,002 appearing on the

TABLE II

ILLUSTRATION OF
A CURRENCY STABILISATION SCHEME

Commodity	Quantity	Currency in which quoted	Price in that currency	Rate of exchange	Price in own currency
Aluminium	x tons	$	.	.	.
Beef	.	£	.	.	.
Camphor	.	Ducats	—	—	.
Cocoa	.	.	.	.	.
Coffee	.	.	.	.	.
Coal	.	.	.	.	.
Coke	.	.	.	.	.
Copper	.	.	.	.	.
Copra	.	.	.	.	.
Corn	.	Ducats	—	—	.
etc.	.	.	.	.	.
				Total	1,000

screen would tell them to contract or tighten controls, i.e. restrict loans by making them dearer or being more selective, and selling other currencies more freely; 997 would tell them that they could slightly relax and expand. (A special write-out of the computer in the chairman's office would currently inform him which of his officers did promptly respond to these instructions.) The effect of this contraction or expansion on commodity prices would be chiefly indirect through the rates of exchange with the currencies in which these commodities were chiefly traded, and direct only with regard to commodities traded chiefly in ducats.

The same signal would appear on the currency exchange and, if the bank was known for taking prompt and effective measures to correct any deviation, would lead to its efforts being assisted by more of its currency being demanded when it was expected to appreciate because its value was below normal (the guide number showing 1,002), and less being demanded when it was expected slightly to depreciate (because the guide number had fallen to 997). It is difficult to see how such a policy consistently pursued would not result in the fluctuations of the value of the currency around the chosen commodity standard being reduced to a very small range indeed.

**

The crucial factor: demand for currency to hold

But, whether directly or indirectly *via* the price of other currencies, it would seem clear that, if an institution acts in the knowledge that the public preparedness to hold its currency, and therefore its business, depends on maintaining the currency value, it will be both able and compelled to assure this result by appropriate continuous adjustments of the quantity in circulation. The crucial point it must keep in mind will be that, to keep a large and growing amount of its currency in circulation, it will be not the demand for *borrowing* it but the willingness of the public to *hold* it that will be decisive. An incautious increase of the current issue may therefore make the flow back to the bank grow faster than the public demand to hold it.

The press, as pointed out, would closely watch the results of the efforts of each issuing bank and daily quote how much the various currencies deviate from the self-set standards. From the point of view of the issuing banks it would probably be desirable to allow a small, previously-announced, tolerance or standard of deviation in either direction. For in that event, and so long as a bank demonstrated its power and resolution to bring rates of exchange (or commodity prices in terms of its currency) promptly back to its standard, speculation would come to its aid and relieve it of the necessity to take precipitate steps to assure absolute stability.

So long as the bank had succeeded in keeping the value of its currency at the desired level, it is difficult to see that it should for this purpose have to contract its circulation so rapidly as to be embarrassed. The usual cause of such developments in the past was circumstances which increased the demand for liquid 'cash', but the bank would have to reduce the aggregate amount outstanding only to adjust it to a shrunken total demand for both forms of its currency. If it had lent mainly on short term, the normal repayment of loans would have brought this result fairly rapidly. The whole matter appears to be very simple and straightforward so long as we assume that all the competing banks try to control their currencies with the aim of keeping their values in some sense constant.

Would competition disrupt the system?

What, however, would be the consequences if one competitor attempted to gain in this competition by offering other ad-

[58]

vantages such as a low rate of interest, or if it granted book credits or perhaps even issued notes (in other words, incurred debts payable on demand) in terms of the currency issued by another bank? Would either practice seriously interfere with the control the issuing banks can exercise over the value of their currencies?

There will of course always be a strong temptation for any bank to try and expand the circulation of its currency by lending cheaper than competing banks; but it would soon discover that, insofar as the additional lending is not based on a corresponding increase of saving, such attempts would inevitably rebound and hurt the bank that over-issued. While people will no doubt be very eager to *borrow* a currency offered at a lower rate of interest, they will not want to *hold* a larger proportion of their liquid assets in a currency of the increased issue of which they would soon learn from various reports and symptoms.

It is true that, so long as the currencies are almost instantaneously exchangeable against one another at a known rate of exchange, the relative prices of commodities in terms of them will also remain the same. Even on the commodity markets the prices of those commodities (or, in regions where a high proportion of the demand is expressed in terms of the increased currency, prices in terms of all currencies) will tend to rise compared with other prices. But the decisive events will take place on the currency exchange. At the prevailing rate of exchange the currency that has increased in supply will constitute a larger proportion of the total of all currencies than people have habitually held. Above all, everybody indebted in the currencies for which a higher rate of interest has to be paid will try to borrow cheap in order to acquire currencies in which he can repay the more burdensome loans. And all the banks that have not reduced their lending rate will promptly return to the bank that lends more cheaply all of its currency they receive. The result must be the appearance on the currency exchange of an excess supply of the over-issued currency, which will quickly bring about a fall in the rate at which it can be exchanged into the others. And it will be at this new rate that commodity prices normally quoted in other currencies will be translated into the offending currency; while, as a result of its over-issue, prices normally quoted in it will be immediately driven up. The fall in the market quotation and the rise of commodity prices in terms of the offending currency would soon induce habitual holders to shift to another currency. The consequent reduction in the demand for it would probably soon more than offset the temporary gain obtained by lending it more cheaply. If the issuing bank nevertheless pursued cheap lending, a general flight from the currency would set in; and continued cheap lending would mean that larger and larger amounts would be dumped on the currency exchange. We can confidently conclude that it would not be possible for a bank to pull down the real value of other currencies by over-issue of its currency—certainly not if their issuers are prepared, so far as necessary, to counter such an attempt by temporarily curtailing their issues.

Would parasitic currencies prevent control of currency value?

A more difficult question, the answer to which is perhaps not so clear, is how far the unavoidable appearance of what one may call parasitic currencies, i.e. the pyramiding of a super-structure of circulating credit through other banks carrying cheque accounts and perhaps even issuing notes in the denomination of the currency of the original issuer, would interfere with the issuer's control over the value of his own currency. So long as such parasitic issues were clearly labelled as debts to be paid in the currency of the issuer it is difficult to see how this could be or should be prevented by law.

Clearly not all banks would wish to issue, or probably could issue, a currency of their own. Those that did not would have no choice but to accept deposits and grant credits in terms of some other currency, and would prefer to do so in the best currency available. Nor would the original issuer wish altogether to prevent this, although he might dislike the issue of notes more than the mere running of accounts subject to cheque in terms of his currency. Notes issued by a secondary issuer would, of course, have to show clearly that they were not the original ducats issued by the bank that owned that trade mark, but merely claims for ducats, since otherwise they would simply be a forgery. Yet I do not see how the ordinary legal protection of brand names or trade marks could prevent the issue of such claims in the form of notes, and very much doubt whether it would be desirable to prevent it by law, especially in view of the essential similarity between such notes and deposits subject to cheque which even the issuing banks would hardly wish to prevent.

What the original issuer of such a currency could do and would have to do is not to repeat the mistakes governments have made, as a result of which control of these secondary or parasitic issues has slipped from their hands. It must make clear that it would not be prepared to bail out secondary issuers by supplying the 'cash' (i.e. the original notes) they will need to redeem their obligations. We shall see later (Section XVI) how governments were led into this trap and allowed their monopoly of the issue of money to be watered down in the most undesirable manner. (They shared the responsibility for control of the total amount of the standard denomination, yielding to the constant pressure for cheap money that was supposed to be met by the rapid spread of banks which they assisted by securing their liquidity; and in the end nobody had full power over the total quantity of money.)

The answer to the most serious problem arising from the scheme seems to me that, though private issuers will have to tolerate the appearance of parasitic circulations of deposits and notes of the same denomination, they ought not to assist but rather restrain it by making it clear in advance that they would not be prepared to provide the notes needed to redeem parasitic issues except against 'hard cash', i.e. by sale against some other reliable currency. By adhering strictly to this principle they would force the secondary issuer to practise something very close to '100 per cent banking'. So far as there would still be limited fiduciary parasitic issues they would have to be kept in circulation by a policy which assured that their value was never questioned. Though this policy might limit the circulation and thus the profit of the original issuer, it should not seriously impair his ability to keep the value of his currency constant.

*

To achieve this the original issuer of a currency with a certain label would have to anticipate the effects of the over-issue of such a parasitic currency (or any other currency claiming to maintain a value equal to its own) and ruthlessly to refuse to buy it at par even before the expected depreciation manifests itself in the rise of some commodity prices in terms of that other currency. The dealings of an issue bank in other currencies would therefore never be a purely mechanical affair (buying and selling at constant prices) guided only by the observed changes in the purchasing power of the other currencies; nor could such a bank undertake to buy any other currency at a rate corresponding to its current buying power over the standard batch of commodities; but it would require a good deal of judgement effectively to defend the short-run stability of one's own currency, and the business will have to be guided in some measure by prediction of the future development of the value of other currencies.

* *

XII. WHICH SORT OF CURRENCY WOULD THE PUBLIC SELECT?

Since it is my thesis that the public would select from a number of competing private currencies a better money than governments provide, I must now examine the process and the criteria by which such a selection would take place.

This is a question on which we have little empirical knowledge. It would be of little use to try asking the people (perhaps by an opinion poll). Never having been in such a position, most people have never thought or formed an opinion about what they would do. We can merely attempt to derive the probable character of individual decisions from our general knowledge of the purpose for which people want money, and the manner in which they act in similar situations. This is, after all, the procedure by which most of economic theory has been built up and has arrived at conclusions usually confirmed by later experience. We must not, of course, assume that people will at once act rationally in a new situation. But, if not by insight, they would soon learn by experience and imitation of the most successful what conduct best serves their interests.[1] A major change like the one considered here might at first cause much uncertainty and confusion. Yet I do not think there is much reason to doubt that people would

[1] Cf. C. Menger [43], p. 261: 'There is no better way in which men can become more enlightened about their economic interests than by observation of the economic success of those who employ the correct means of achieving their ends.'

soon discover what rational consideration could have told them at once. Whether in practice the process would be fast or slow may differ from country to country.[1]

Four uses of money

There are four kinds of uses of money that would chiefly affect the choice among available kinds of currency: its use, first, for cash purchases of commodities and services, second, for holding reserves for future needs, third, in contracts for deferred payments, and, finally, as a unit of account, especially in keeping books. To treat these uses as different 'functions' of money is common but not really expedient. They are in effect simply consequences of the basic function of money as a medium of exchange, and will only in exceptional conditions, such as a rapid depreciation of the medium of exchange, come to be separated from it. They are also interdependent in such a way that, although at first different attributes of money may seem desirable for its different uses, money renders one service, namely that as a unit of account, which makes stability of value the most desirable of all. Although at first convenience in daily purchases might be thought decisive in the selection, I believe it would prove that suitability as a unit of account would rule the roost.

(i) Cash purchases

To the great mass of wage- and salary-earners the chief interest will probably be that they can make their daily purchases in the currency in which they are paid, and that they find prices everywhere indicated in the currency they use. Shopkeepers, on the other hand, so long as they know they can instantaneously exchange any currency at a known rate of exchange against any other, would be only too willing to accept any currency at an appropriate price. Electronic cash registers would probably be developed rapidly, not only to show instantaneously the equivalent of any price in any

[1] We must not entirely overlook the possibility that the practices and expectations of business men based on past experience, and particularly the experience of the last fifty years or so, are so much adjusted to the probability of a continuous upward trend of prices, that the realisation that average prices in future are likely to remain constant may at first have a discouraging effect. This may even make some business men prefer to deal and keep accounts in a slowly depreciating currency. I believe, however, that in the end those who have chosen a stable currency will prove more successful.

currency desired, but also to be connected through the computer with banks so that firms would immediately be credited with the equivalent in the currency in which they kept their accounts. (Cash balances in the currencies would be collected every evening.) On the other hand, shopkeepers would find it expedient, if two or three currencies were in common local use, to mark their wares in an easily distinguishable manner, for example in different colours for each currency, so as to ease price comparisons between shops and currencies.

(ii) *Holding reserves for future payments*

Beyond the desire to use his regular receipts for his ordinary expenditure, the wage- and salary-earner would probably be interested chiefly in stability. And although in his mortgage and instalment payments he might for a while profit from a depreciating currency, his wage or salary contract would incline his wishes towards an appreciating currency.

All holders of cash, that is, everybody, would prefer an appreciating currency and for this reason there might be a substantial demand for such money; but it would clearly not be to the advantage of borrowers to borrow in it, or for banks to have to maintain a value higher than that at which they issued a currency. It is conceivable that a limited amount of notes of such an appreciating currency might be issued and used for special purposes, but it would seem most unlikely that they would become generally used. The chief demand for holding would probably be for the currency in which people expected to have to pay debts.

(iii) *Standard of deferred payments*

When we come to the third use, as a standard of deferred payments, the primary interests of the parties to the contract would of course be precisely opposite: lenders preferring an appreciating and borrowers a depreciating currency. But each group would be of a very mixed composition, the creditors including all wage- and salary-earners as well as the owners of capital, and the debtors including the banks as well as enterprises and farmers. It therefore seems unlikely that market forces would produce a predominant bias in one direction. And, though they would all in the short run either lose or gain from changes in the value of the currency on their borrowing or lending business, they would probably all soon discover

[64]

that these losses or gains were merely temporary and tended to disappear as soon as interest rates adapted themselves to expected price movements.

(iv) *A reliable unit of account*
It seems to me that the decisive factor that would create a general preference for a currency stable in value would be that only in such a currency is a realistic calculation possible, and therefore in the long run a successful choice between alternative currencies for use in production and trade. In particular, the chief task of accounting, to ensure that the stock of capital of the business is not eaten into and only true net gains shown as profits available for disposal by the shareholders, can be realised only if the value of the unit of account is approximately stable.

An attempt to explain further why successful economic calculation is possible only with a stable value of money raises the question of what precisely we mean by 'the value of money' and the various respects in which it may be kept stable. This we must leave to Section XIII. For the present we content ourselves with the empirical fact that effective capital maintenance and cost control is possible only if accounts are kept in a unit that in some sense remains tolerably stable. So we will provisionally leave the present subject with the conclusion that, in the long run at least, the effective choice between competitive offers of currencies will be the usual one of competition. The currency that will prevail will be the one preferred by the people who are helped to succeed and who in consequence will be imitated by others.

XIII. WHICH VALUE OF MONEY?

Strictly speaking, in a scientific sense, there is no such thing as a perfectly stable value of money—or of anything else. Value is a relationship, a rate of equivalence, or, as W. S. Jevons said, 'an indirect mode of expressing a ratio',[1] which can be stated only by naming the quantity of one object that is valued

---

[1] W. S. Jevons [34], p. 11. Cf. also *ibid.*, p. 68: 'Value merely expresses the essentially variable ratio in which two commodities exchange, so that there is no reason to suppose that any substance does for two days together retain the same value.'

equally with the 'equivalent' quantity of another object. Two objects may keep a constant relative value in terms of each other, but unless we specify the other, the statement that the value of something is unchanged has no definite meaning.

What we mean when we habitually but carelessly use such expressions as 'Beer is more stable in value than beetroot' (and this is the most we can ever assert with any meaning) is that the relative value of beer, or its rate of exchange, tends to remain more stable with a larger number of other goods or over longer periods, than is true of beetroot and many other goods. For ordinary goods or services we have in mind in the first instance usually their relation to money. When we apply the term 'value' to money itself what is meant is that the price of most commodities will not tend to change predominantly in one direction, or will change only little, over short periods.

'A stable value of money'

But some prices always change on a free market. We will sometimes feel that the value of money has remained approximately constant although many prices have changed, and at other times that the value of money has definitely decreased or increased, although the prices of only a few important commodities have changed but all in the same direction. What then do we call, in a world of constantly changing individual prices, a stable value of money?

In a rough sense it is of course fairly obvious that the command over commodities in general conferred by a sum of money has decreased if it brings a smaller amount of most of them and more of only a few of them. It is then sensible to say that the command over commodities has remained about the same if these two changes in command over commodities just balance. But for our purposes we need, of course, a more precise definition of 'a stable value of money' and a more exact definition of the benefits we expect from it.

Balancing errors

As we have seen, the chief disturbances which changes in the value of money will cause operate through the effects on contracts for deferred payments and on the use of money units as the basis of calculation and accounting. Decisions in both have to cope with the unalterable truth that for the individual the future movement of most prices is unpredictable (because

[66]

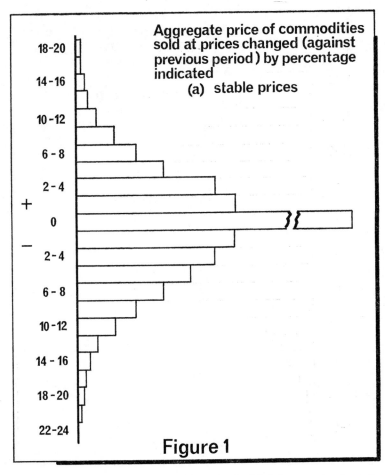

Figure 1

they serve as signals of events of most of which he cannot know). The resulting risk can best be reduced by basing calculations on expectations of future prices from which current prices are quite as likely to deviate in the one direction as in the other by any given percentage. This median value of probable future changes will be correctly estimated only if it is zero and thus coincides with the probable behaviour of the large number of prices that are fairly rigid or sluggish (chiefly public utility rates but also the prices of most branded articles, goods sold by mail order houses, and the like).

The position is best illustrated by two diagrams. If the value of money is so regulated that an appropriate average of prices is kept constant, the probabilities of future price movements

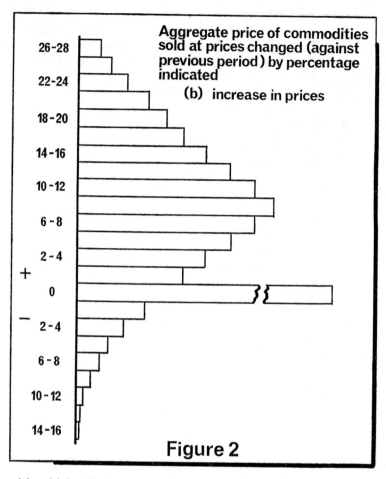

Figure 2

with which all planning of future activities will have to cope
can be represented as in Figure I. Though in this case the
unpredictability of particular future prices, inevitable in a
functioning market economy, remains, the fairly high long-run
chances are that for people in general the effects of the unforeseen price changes will just about cancel out. They will at least
not cause a general error of expectations in one direction but on
the whole make fairly successful calculations based on the
assumption of the continuance of prices (where no better
information is available).

Where the divergent movement of individual prices results
in a *rise* in the average of all prices, it will look somewhat as
in Figure 2.

Since the individual enterprise will have as little foundation for correctly foreseeing the median of all the movements as for predicting the movements of individual prices, it could also not base its calculations and decisions on a known median from which individual movements of prices were as likely to diverge in the one direction as in the other. Successful calculations, or effective capital and cost accounting, would then become impossible. People would more and more wish for a unit of account whose value moved more closely together with the general trend, and might even be driven to use as the unit of account something that could not be used as a medium of exchange.[1]

Criteria of choice

These skewed shifts of the distribution of price changes to one side of constancy which changes in the quantity of money may cause, and the resulting difficulty of foresight, calculation and accounting, must not be confused with the merely temporary changes in the structure of relative prices the same process also brings about which will cause misdirections of production. We shall have to consider (Section XVII) how a stabilisation of the value of money will also substantially prevent those misdirections of production which later inevitably lead to reversals of the process of growth, the loss of much investment, and periods of unemployment. We shall argue that this would

[1] The curve representing the dispersion of price changes by showing the percentage of all sales effected at one period at prices increased or decreased compared with an earlier period would, of course, if drawn on a logarithmic scale, have the same shape whether we used money or any commodity as the measure of price. If we used as standard the commodity whose price had fallen more than that of any other, all price changes would merely appear as increases, but an increase of the relative price compared with that of another would still be shown as, say, a 50 per cent increase, whatever measure we used. We would probably obtain a curve of the general shape of a normal (Gaussian) curve of error—the, so far as we could have predicted, accidental deviations from the mode on either side just offsetting each other and becoming less numerous as the deviations increase. (Most price changes will be due to a shifting of demand with corresponding falls of some prices and rises of others; and relatively small transfers of this kind seem likely to be more frequent than large ones.) In terms of a money with stable value in this sense, the price of the commodities represented by the mode would then be unchanged, while the amount of transactions taking place at prices increased or decreased by a certain percentage would just balance each other. This will minimise errors, not necessarily of particular individuals, but in the aggregate. And though no practicable index number can fully achieve what we have assumed, a close approximation to the effect ought to be possible.

be one of the chief benefits of a stable currency. But it is hardly possible to argue that the users of money will for this reason select a currency with a stable value. This is an effect they are not likely to perceive and take into account in their individual decision of what money to use—although the observation of the smooth course of business in regions using a stable currency may induce the people of other regions to prefer a similar currency. The individual also could not protect himself against this effect by himself using a stable currency, because the structure of relative prices will be the same in terms of the different concurrent currencies and those distortions cannot therefore be avoided so long as side by side with stable currencies fluctuating currencies are used to a significant extent.

The reason why people will tend to prefer a currency with a value stable in terms of commodities will thus be that it will help them to minimise the effects of the unavoidable uncertainty about price movements because the effect of errors in opposite directions will tend to cancel each other out. This cancelling will not take place if the median around which the deviation of individual prices clusters is not zero but some unknown magnitude. Even if we agree that the stable money people will prefer to use will be such that they expect the individual prices in which they are chiefly interested to be as likely to increase in terms of it as to decrease, this does not yet tell us which price level most people will want to see constant. Different people or enterprises will evidently be interested in the prices of different commodities. And the aggregate prices of different collections of commodities would of course move differently.

Effectiveness for accounting again decisive

While one probably is at first again inclined to think in terms of retail prices or cost of living, and even most individual consumers might prefer a money stable in these terms, it is not likely that an extensive circulation could be built up for a currency so regulated. The cost of living differs from place to place and is apt to change at varying rates. Business would certainly prefer a money acceptable over wide regions. What would be most important for calculation and accounting in each enterprise (and therefore for the efficient use of resources), relying on the general stability of prices rather than its specialised knowledge of a particular market, would be the prices of widely traded products such as raw materials, agricultural foodstuffs and certain standardised semi-finished industrial products. They have the further advantage that they are traded on regular markets, their prices are promptly reported and, at least with raw materials, are particularly sensitive and would therefore make it possible by early action to forestall tendencies towards general price movements (which often show themselves in such commodities first).

*

Indeed it may well be that a regulation of the issue which directly aimed at stabilising raw material prices might result in a greater stability even of the prices of consumers' goods than a management which aimed directly at the latter object. The considerable lag which experience has shown to prevail between changes in the quantity of money and changes in the price level of consumers' goods may indeed mean that, if adjustment of circulation were postponed until the effects of an excess or shortage of the issue showed itself in changes in the prices of consumers' goods, quite noticeable changes in their prices could not be avoided; while, in the case of raw materials, where this lag seems to be shorter, an earlier warning would make prompter precautionary measures possible.

**

Wage- and salary-earners would probably also discover that it was advantageous to conclude collective bargains in average raw material prices or a similar magnitude, which would secure for earners of fixed incomes an automatic share in an increase of industrial productivity. (The underdeveloped countries would also prefer an international currency that gave raw materials in general an increasing purchasing power over industrial products—though they are likely to spoil the possibility by insisting on the stabilisation of individual raw material prices.) I hope, at any rate, that this will be the predominant choice because a currency stable in terms of raw material prices is probably also the nearest approach we can hope to achieve to one conducive to stability of general economic activity.

Wholesale commodity prices as standard of value
for currencies over international regions
My expectation would be that, at least for large regions much exceeding present national territories, people would agree on

a standard set of wholesale prices of commodities to treat as the standard of value in which they would prefer to have their currencies kept constant. A few banks that had established wide circulation by accommodating this preference, and issued currencies of different denominations but with roughly constant rates of exchange with one another, might continue to try and refine the precise composition of the standard 'basket' of commodities whose price they tried to keep constant in their currency.[1] But this practice would not cause substantial fluctuations in the relative values of the chief currencies circulating in the region. Regions with different compositions of the currencies in circulation would, of course, overlap, and currencies whose value was based chiefly on commodities important for one way of life, or for one group of predominant industries, might fluctuate relatively more against others but yet retain their distinct clientele among people with particular occupations and habits.

XIV. THE USELESSNESS OF THE QUANTITY THEORY FOR OUR PURPOSES

The usual assumptions of monetary theory, that there is only one kind of currency, *the* money, and that there is no sharp distinction between full money and mere money substitutes, thus disappear. So does the applicability of what is called the quantity theory of the value of money—even as a rough approximation to a theoretically more satisfactory explanation of the determination of the value of money, which is all that it can ever be.[2]

The quantity theory presupposes, of course, that there is only one kind of money in circulation within a given territory, the quantity of which can be ascertained by counting its homogeneous (or near-homogeneous) units. But if the different currencies in circulation within a region have no constant

---

[1] Indeed emulation would probably lead them to refine the technique for maintaining maximum stability to a point far beyond any practical advantage.

[2] But, as I wrote 45 years ago [24, p. 3] and would still maintain, '. . . from a practical point of view, it would be one of the worst things which could befall us if the general public should ever again cease to believe in the elementary propositions of the quantity theory'.

relative value, the aggregate amount in circulation can only be derived from the relative value of the currencies and has no meaning apart from it. A theory which is of use only in a particular situation, even if it happened to prevail during a long period, evidently suffers from a serious defect. Though we are apt to take it for granted, it is by no means of the essence of money that within a given territory there should exist only one kind, and it is usually true only because governments have prevented the use of other kinds. Even so, it is never fully true because there are always significant differences in the demand for different forms of money and money substitutes of varying degrees of liquidity. But if we assume that issuers of currency continually compete with one another for additional users of their currency, we cannot also assume, as the quantity theory can assume with some justification with respect to a currency of a single denomination, that there exists a fairly constant demand for money in the sense that the aggregate value of the total stock will tend to be approximately constant (or change in a predictable manner with the size of the population, the gross national product, or similar magnitudes).

The cash balance approach . . .

For the problems discussed in this *Paper* we certainly require a more generally applicable tool. It is fortunately available in the form of a theory which is more satisfactory even for dealing with the simpler situations: the cash balance approach deriving from Carl Menger, Leon Walras and Alfred Marshall. It enables us not merely to explain the ultimate effect of changes in 'the quantity of money' on 'the' general price level, but also to account for the process by which changes in the supplies of various kinds of money will successively affect different prices. It makes possible an analysis which admittedly cannot pretend to the pseudo-exactness of the quantity theory, but which has a much wider reach and can take account of the preferences of individuals for different kinds of money.

The decisive consideration to keep in mind for our present purpose is that in a multi-currency system there is no such thing as *the* magnitude of the demand for money. There will be different demands for the different kinds of currency; but since these different currencies will not be perfect substitutes, these distinct demands cannot be added up into a single sum. There may be little demand for (but large supply of) depreciating currencies, there will, we hope, be an equality of demand and supply for stable currencies (which is what will keep their values stable), and a large demand for (but little supply of) appreciating currencies. Though, so long as there exists a free market for currencies, people will be prepared to *sell* (at some price) for any currency, they will not be prepared to *hold* any currency; and the character of the available substitutes would affect the demand for any particular currency. There would therefore be no single quantity the magnitude of which could be said to be decisive for the value of money.

. . . and the velocity of circulation

It can be maintained that the analyses in terms of the demand for cash balances and the use of the concept of velocity of circulation by the quantity theory are formally equivalent. The difference is important. The cash balance approach directs attention to the crucial causal factor, the individuals' desire for holding stocks of money. The velocity of circulation refers to a resultant statistical magnitude which experience may show to be fairly constant over the fairly long periods for which we have useful data—thus providing some justification for claiming a simple connection between 'the' quantity of money and 'the' price level—but which is often misleading because it becomes so easily associated with the erroneous belief that monetary changes affect only the *general* level of prices. They are then often regarded as harmful chiefly for this reason, as if they raised or lowered all prices *simultaneously* and by the *same* percentage. Yet the real harm they do is due to the *differential* effect on different prices, which change successively in a very irregular order and to a very different degree, so that as a result the whole structure of relative prices becomes distorted and misguides production into wrong directions.

Unfortunately, Lord Keynes made practically no use of this most important contribution to monetary theory of the Cambridge tradition deriving from Marshall. Though criticising the alleged tendency of all contemporary monetary theory to argue as if prices all changed simultaneously, he moved almost entirely within the framework of (or argued against) the Irving Fisher type of quantity theory. It is one of the chief damages the Keynesian flood has done to the understanding of the economic process that the comprehension of the factors determining both the value of money and the effects of monetary events on the value of particular commodities has been largely lost. I cannot attempt here even a concentrated restatement of this central chapter of monetary theory but must content myself with recommending economists who have had the misfortune to study monetary theory at institutions wholly dominated by Keynesian views but who still wish to understand the theory of the value of money to fill this gap by first working through the two volumes of A. W. Marget's *Theory of Prices* [42] and then skip most of the literature of the next 25 years until Professor Axel Leijonhufvud's recent book [37],[1] which will guide them to works of the interval they ought not to miss.

*

A note on 'monetarism'

It has become usual, since the reaction against the dominance of the 'Keynesian' dogma set in, to lump together as 'monetarists' all who regard as mistaken Keynes's denial 'that an inflationary or deflationary movement was normally caused or necessarily accompanied' by 'changes in the quantity of money and velocity of its circulation'.[2] This 'monetarism' is of course a view held before Keynes by almost all economists except a very few dissenters and cranks, including in particular those Continental economists who by their advice on policy became responsible for the great inflations of the 1920s. I agree with these 'monetarists' in particular on what is now probably regarded as their defining characteristic, namely that they believe that all inflation is what is now called 'demand-pull' inflation, and that there is, so far as the economic mechanism is concerned, no such thing as a 'cost-push' inflation—unless one treats as part of the economic causation the political decision to increase the quantity of money in response to a rise of wages which otherwise would cause unemployment.[3]

[1] [A short guide to Professor Leijonhufvud's book is his *Keynes and the Classics*, Occasional Paper 30, IEA, 1969 (6th Impression, 1977).—ED.]

[2] R. F. Harrod [23a, p. 513].

[3] In another sense I stand, however, outside the Keynes-monetarists controversy: both are macro-economic approaches to the problem, while I believe that

[*Contd. on page 76*]

[75]

Where I differ from the majority of other 'monetarists' and in particular from the leading representative of the school, Professor Milton Friedman, is that I regard the simple quantity theory of money, even for situations where in a given territory only one kind of money is employed, as no more than a useful rough approximation to a really adequate explanation, which, however, becomes wholly useless where several concurrent distinct kinds of money are simultaneously in use in the same territory. Though this defect becomes serious only with the multiplicity of concurrent currencies which we are considering here, the phenomenon of substitution of things not counted as money by the theory for what is counted as money by it always impairs the strict validity of its conclusions.

Its chief defect in any situation seems to me to be that by its stress on the effects of changes in the quantity of money on the general level of prices it directs all-too exclusive attention to the harmful effects of inflation and deflation on the creditor-debtor relationship, but disregards the even more important and harmful effects of the injections and withdrawals of amounts of money from circulation on the structure of relative prices and the consequent misallocation of resources and particularly the misdirection of investments which it causes.

This is not an appropriate place for a full discussion of the fine points of theory on which there exist considerable differences within the 'monetarist' school, though they are of great importance for the evaluation of the effects of the present

[Contd. from page 75]

monetary theory neither needs nor ought to employ such an approach, even if it can hardly wholly dispense with such an essentially macro-economic concept. Macro-economics and micro-economics are alternative methods of dealing with the difficulty that, in the case of such a complex phenomenon as the market, we never command all the factual information which we would need to provide a full explanation. Macro-economics attempts to overcome this difficulty by referring to such magnitudes as aggregates or averages which are statistically available. This gives us a useful approximation to the facts, but as a theoretical explanation of causal connections is unsatisfactory and sometimes misleading, because it asserts empirically observed correlations with no justification for the belief that they will always occur.

The alternative micro-economic approach which I prefer relies on the construction of models which cope with the problem raised by our inescapable ignorance of all the relevant facts by 'reducing the scale' by diminishing the number of independent variables to the minimum required to form a structure which is capable of producing all the *kinds* of movements or changes of which a market system is capable. It is, as I have tried to explain more fully elsewhere [30], a technique which produces merely what I have called 'pattern' predictions but is incapable of producing those predictions of specific events which macro-economics claims, as I believe mistakenly, to be able to produce.

proposals. My fundamental objection to the adequacy of the pure quantity theory of money is that, even with a single currency in circulation within a territory, there is, strictly speaking, no such thing as *the* quantity of money, and that any attempt to delimit certain groups of the media of exchange expressed in terms of a single unit as if they were homogeneous or perfect substitutes is misleading even for the usual situation. This objection becomes of decisive importance, of course, when we contemplate different concurrent currencies.

A stable price level and a high and stable level of employment do not require or permit the total quantity of money to be kept constant or to change at a constant rate. It demands something similar yet still significantly different, namely that the quantity of money (or rather the aggregate value of all the most liquid assets) be kept such that people will not reduce or increase their outlay for the purpose of adapting their balances to their altered liquidity preferences. Keeping the quantity of money constant does not assure that the money stream will remain constant, and in order to make the volume of the money stream behave in a desired manner the supply of money must possess considerable elasticity.

Monetary management cannot aim at a particular predetermined volume of circulation, not even in the case of a territorial monopolist of issue, and still less in the case of competing issues, but only at finding out what quantity will keep prices constant. No authority can beforehand ascertain, and only the market can discover, the 'optimal quantity of money'. It can be provided only by selling and buying at a fixed price the collection of commodities the aggregate price of which we wish to keep stable.

As regards Professor Friedman's proposal of a legal limit on the rate at which a monopolistic issuer of money was to be allowed to increase the quantity in circulation, I can only say that I would not like to see what would happen if under such a provision it ever became known that the amount of cash in circulation was approaching the upper limit and that therefore a need for increased liquidity could not be met.[1]

---

[1] To such a situation the classic account of Walter Bagehot [3, penultimate paragraph] would apply: 'In a sensitive state of the English money market the near approach to the legal limit of reserve would be a sure incentive to panic; if one-third were fixed by law, the moment the banks were close to one-third, alarm would begin and would run like magic.'

Why indexation is not a substitute for a stable currency

The usual emphasis on the most generally perceived and most painfully felt harm done by inflation, its effect on debtor-creditor relations and in particular on the receivers of fixed incomes, has led to the suggestion that these effects be mitigated by stipulating long-term obligations in terms of a 'tabular standard', the nominal sum of the debt being continuously corrected according to the changes in an index number of prices. It is, of course, correct that such a practice would eliminate the most glaring injustices caused by inflation and would remove the most severe suffering visibly due to it. But these are far from being the most severe damage which inflation causes, and the adoption of such a partial remedy for some of the symptoms would probably weaken the resistance against inflation, thus prolonging and increasing it, and in the long run considerably magnify the damage it causes and particularly the suffering it produces by bringing about unemployment.

Everybody knows of course that inflation does not affect all prices at the same time but makes different prices rise in succession, and that it therefore changes the relation between prices—although the familiar statistics of *average* price movements tend to conceal this movement in *relative* prices. The effect on relative incomes is only one, though to the superficial observer the most conspicuous, effect of the distortion of the whole structure of relative prices. What is in the long run even more damaging to the functioning of the economy and eventually tends to make a free market system unworkable is the effect of this distorted price structure in misdirecting the use of resources and drawing labour and other factors of production (especially the investment of capital) into uses which remain profitable only so long as inflation accelerates. It is this effect which produces the major waves of unemployment,[1] but which

[1] A remarkable recognition of this fundamental truth occurs in the opening paragraphs of the final communique of the Downing Street 'summit' meeting of 8 May, 1977, chaired by the Prime Minister of the UK and attended by the President of the USA, the Chancellor of West Germany, the President of France, the Prime Minister of Japan and the Prime Minister of Italy. The first few lines said: 'Inflation is not a remedy for unemployment, but is one of its major causes'. This is an insight for which I have been fighting, almost single-handed, for more than forty years. Unfortunately, however, that statement over-simplified the issue. In many circumstances inflation indeed leads to a *temporary* reduction of unemployment, but only at the price of causing much more unemployment later. This is exactly what makes inflation so seductive and politically almost irresistible, but for that reason particularly insidious.

the economists using a macro-economic approach to the problem usually neglect or underrate.

This crucial damage done by inflation would in no way be eliminated by indexation. Indeed, government measures of this sort, which make it easier to live with inflation, must in the long run make things worse. They would certainly not make it easier to fight inflation, because people would be less aware that their suffering was due to inflation. There is no justification for Professor Friedman's suggestion that

'by removing distortions in relative prices produced by inflation, widespread escalator clauses would make it easier for the public to recognise changes in the rate of inflation, would thereby reduce the time-lag in adapting to such changes, and thus make the nominal price level more sensitive and variable.'[1]

Such inflation, with some of its visible effect mitigated, would clearly be less resisted and last correspondingly longer.

It is true that Professor Friedman explicitly disclaims any suggestion that indexation is a substitute for stable money,[2] but he attempts to make it more tolerable in the short run and I regard any such endeavour as exceedingly dangerous. In spite of his denial it seems to me that to some degree it would even speed up inflation. It would certainly strengthen the claims of groups of workers whose real wages ought to fall (because their kind of work has become less valuable) to have their real wages kept constant. But that means that all relative increases of any wages relatively to any others would have to find expression in an increase of the nominal wages of all except those workers whose wages were the lowest, and this itself would make continuous inflation necessary.

It seems to me, in other words, like any other attempts to accept wage and price rigidities as inevitable and to adjust monetary policy to them, the attitude from which 'Keynesian' economics took its origin, to be one of those steps apparently dictated by practical necessity but bound in the long run to make the whole wage structure more and more rigid and thereby lead to the destruction of the market economy. But the present political necessity ought to be no concern of the economic scientist. His task ought to be, as I will not cease

[1] M. Friedman [20b], p. 31.

[2] *Ibid.*, p. 28.

repeating, to make politically possible what today may be politically impossible. To decide what can be done at the moment is the task of the politician, not of the economist, who must continue to point out that to persist in this direction will lead to disaster.

I am in complete agreement with Professor Friedman on the inevitability of inflation under the existing political and financial institutions. But I believe that it will lead to the destruction of our civilisation unless we change the political framework. In this sense I will admit that my radical proposal concerning money will probably be practicable only as part of a much more far-reaching change in our political institutions, but an essential part of such a reform which will be recognised as necessary before long. The two distinct reforms which I am proposing in the economic and the political order[1] are indeed complementary: the sort of monetary system I propose may be possible only under a limited government such as we do not have, and a limitation of government may require that it be deprived of the monopoly of issuing money. Indeed the latter should necessarily follow from the former.

The historical evidence

Professor Friedman has since[2] more fully explained his doubts about the efficacy of my proposal and claimed that

'we have ample empirical and historical evidence that suggests that [my] hopes would not in fact be realised—that private currencies which offer purchasing power security would not drive out governmental currencies.'

I can find no such evidence that anything like a currency of which the public has learnt to understand that the issuer can continue his business only if he maintains its currency constant, for which all the usual banking facilities are provided and which is legally recognised as an instrument for contracts, accounting and calculation has not been preferred to a deteriorating official currency, simply because such a situation seems never to have existed. It may well be that in many countries the issue of such a currency is not actually prohibited, but the other conditions are rarely if ever satisfied. And everybody knows that if such a private experiment promised to succeed, governments would at once step in to prevent it.

[1] F. A. Hayek [31a], vol. III.

[2] In an interview given to *Reason* magazine, IX: 34, New York, August 1977, p. 28.

If we want historical evidence of what people will do where they have free choice of the currency they prefer to use, the displacement of sterling as the general unit of international trade since it began continuously to depreciate seems to me strongly to confirm my expectations. What we know about the behaviour of individuals having to cope with a bad national money, and in the face of government using every means at its disposal to force them to use it, all points to the probable success of any money which has the properties the public wants if people are not artificially deterred from using it. Americans may be fortunate in never having experienced a time when everybody in their country regarded some national currency other than their own as safer. But on the European Continent there were many occasions in which, if people had only been permitted, they would have used dollars rather than their national currencies. They did in fact do so to a much larger extent than was legally permitted, and the most severe penalties had to be threatened to prevent this habit from spreading rapidly—witness the billions of unaccounted-for dollar notes undoubtedly held in private hands all over the world.

I have never doubted that the public at large would be slow in recognising the advantages of such a new currency and have even suggested that at first, if given the opportunity, the masses would turn to gold rather than any form of other paper money. But as always the success of the few who soon recognise the advantages of a really stable currency would in the end induce the others to imitate them.

I must confess, however, that I am somewhat surprised that Professor Friedman of all people should have so little faith that competition will make the better instrument prevail when he seems to have no ground to believe that monopoly will ever provide a better one and merely fears the indolence produced by old habits.

**

XV. THE DESIRABLE BEHAVIOUR OF THE SUPPLY OF CURRENCY

We have so far provisionally assumed that the kind of money individuals will prefer to use will also be most conducive to the smooth functioning of the market process as a whole. Although this is plausible and, as we shall see, approximately true in practice, it is not self-evident. We have still to examine the validity of this belief. It is at least conceivable that the use of one particular kind of currency might be most convenient for each separate individual but that each might be better off if all the others used a different kind.

We have seen (Section XIII) that successful economic action (or the fulfilment of the expectations which prompted it) depends largely on the approximately correct prediction of future prices. These predictions will be based on current prices and the estimation of their trend, but future prices must always be to some degree uncertain because the circumstances which determine them will be unknown to most individuals. Indeed, the function of prices is precisely to communicate, as rapidly as possible, signals of changes of which the individual cannot know but to which his plans must be adjusted. This system works because on the whole current prices are fairly reliable indications of what future prices will probably be, subject only to those 'accidental' deviations which, as we have seen, if average prices remain constant, are likely to offset each other. We have also seen how such an offsetting of opposite disappointments becomes impossible if a substantial general movement of prices in one direction takes place.

But the current prices of particular commodities or groups of commodities can also be positively misleading if they are caused by non-recurring events, such as temporary inflows or outflows of money to the system. For such apparent changes in demand from a particular direction are in a peculiar manner self-reversing: they systematically channel productive efforts into directions where they cannot be maintained. The most important recurrent misdirections of the use of resources of this sort occur when, by the creation (or withdrawal) of amounts of money, the funds available for investment are increased substantially above (or decreased substantially below) the amounts currently transferred from consumption to investment, or saved.

Although this is the mechanism by which recurrent crises and depressions are caused, it is not a specific effect of a particular kind of currency which the users are likely to be aware of and which might therefore lead them to switch to another. We can expect the selection of the currency they use to be influenced only by such attributes as recognisably affect their actions, but not by indirect effects of changes of its amount which will operate largely through their effects on the decisions of others.

The supply of currency, stable prices, and the equivalence of investment and saving

While the modern author who first drew attention to the crucial importance of these divergences between investment and saving, Knut Wicksell, believed that they would disappear if the value of money were kept constant, this has unfortunately proved to be not strictly correct. It is now generally recognised that even those additions to the quantity of money that in a growing economy are necessary to secure a *stable* price level may cause an excess of investment over saving. But though I was among those who early pointed out this difficulty,[1] I am inclined to believe that it is a problem of minor practical significance. If increases or decreases of the quantity of money never exceeded the amount necessary to keep average prices approximately constant, we would come as close to a condition in which investment approximately corresponded to saving as we are likely to do by any conceivable method. Compared, anyhow, with the divergences between investment and saving which necessarily accompany the major swings in the price level, those which would still occur under a stable price level would probably be of an order of magnitude about which we need not worry.

'Neutral money' fictitious

My impression is that economists have become somewhat over-ambitious concerning the degree of stability that is either achievable or even desirable under any conceivable economic order, and that they have unfortunately encouraged political demands concerning the certainty of employment at a hoped-for wage which in the long run no government can satisfy. That perfect matching or correspondence of the individual plans, which the theoretical model of a perfect market equilibrium derives on the assumption that the money required to make indirect exchange possible has no influence on relative prices, is a wholly fictitious picture to which nothing in the real world can ever correspond. Although I have myself given currency to the expression 'neutral money' (which, as I discovered later, I

[1] Hayek [25], pp. 114 ff.

[83]

had unconsciously borrowed from Wicksell), it was intended to describe this almost universally made assumption of theoretical analysis and to raise the question whether any real money could ever possess this property, and not as a model to be aimed at by monetary policy.[1] I have long since come to the conclusion that no real money can ever be neutral in this sense, and that we must be content with a system that rapidly corrects the inevitable errors. The nearest approach to such a condition which we can hope to achieve would appear to me to be one in which the average prices of the 'original factors of production' were kept constant. But as the average price of land and labour is hardly something for which we can find a statistical measure, the nearest practicable approximation would seem to be precisely that stability of raw material and perhaps other wholesale prices which we could hope competitively issued currencies would secure.

I will readily admit that such a provisional solution (on which the experimentation of competition might gradually improve), though giving us an infinitely better money and much more general economic stability than we have ever had, leaves open various questions to which I have no ready answer. But it seems to meet the most urgent needs much better than any prospects that seemed to exist while one did not contemplate the abolition of the monopoly of the issue of money and the free admission of competition into the business of providing currency.

Increased demand for liquidity

To dispel one kind of doubt which I myself at one stage entertained about the possibility of maintaining a stable price level, we may briefly consider here what would happen if at one time most members of a community wished to keep a much larger proportion of their assets in a highly liquid form than they did before. Would this not justify, and even require, that the value of the most liquid assets, that is, of all money, should rise compared with that of commodities?

The answer is that such needs of all individuals could be met not only by increasing the *value* of the existing liquid assets, money, but also by increasing the *amounts* they can hold. The wish of each individual to have a larger share of his resources

[1] Hayek [26].

[84]

in a very liquid form can be taken care of by additions to the total stock of money. This, paradoxically, increases the sum of the value to the individuals of all existing assets and thereby also the share of them that is highly liquid. Nothing, of course, can increase the liquidity of a closed community as a whole, if that concept has any meaning whatsoever, except, perhaps, if one wishes to extend its meaning to a shift from the production of highly specific to very versatile goods which would increase the ease of adaptation to unforeseen events.

There is no need to be afraid of spurious demands for more money on the ground that more money is needed to secure adequate liquidity. The amount required of any currency will always be that which can be issued or kept in circulation without causing an increase or decrease of the aggregate (direct or indirect) price of the 'basket' of commodities supposed to remain constant. This rule will satisfy all legitimate demands that the variable 'needs of trade' be satisfied. And this will be true in so far as the stated collection of goods can be bought or sold at the stated aggregate price, and the absorption or release of currency from cash balances does not interfere with this condition.

*

It remains true, however, that so long as good and bad currencies circulate side by side, the individual cannot wholly protect himself from the harmful effects of the bad currencies by using only the good ones in his own transactions. Since the relative prices of the different commodities must be the same in terms of the different concurrent currencies, the user of a stable currency cannot escape the effects of the distortion of the price structure by the inflation (or deflation) of a widely used competing currency. The benefit of a stable course of the economic activities which, we shall argue, the use of a stable money would produce, would therefore be achieved only if the great majority of transactions were effected in stable currencies. Such a displacement of most bad money by good would, I believe, come about fairly soon, but occasional disturbances of the whole price structure and in consequence of general economic activity cannot be wholly excluded until the public has learnt rapidly to reject tempting offers of cheap money.

**

[85]

XVI. FREE BANKING

Some of the problems we are encountering were discussed extensively in the course of a great debate on 'free banking' during the middle of the last century, mainly in France and Germany.[1] This debate turned on the question whether commercial banks should have the right to issue bank notes redeemable in the established national gold or silver currency. Bank notes were then very much more important than the scarcely yet developed use of chequing accounts which became important only after (and in part perhaps because) the commercial banks were in the end definitely denied the right to issue bank notes. This outcome of the debate resulted in the establishment in all European countries of a single bank privileged by government to issue notes. (The United States followed only in 1914.)

A single national currency, not several competing currencies

It should be specially observed that the demand for free banking at that time was wholly a demand that the commercial banks should be allowed to issue notes in terms of the single established national currency. So far as I am aware, the possibility of competing banks issuing *different* currencies was never contemplated. That was of course a consequence of the view that only bank notes redeemable in gold or silver were practicable, and therefore that notes for other than the standard quantity of precious metal would seem to be merely inconvenient and not serve any useful purpose.

*

The older legitimate argument for freedom of the note issue by banks became, however, invalid once the notes they issued were no longer to be redeemed in gold or silver, for the supply of which each individual bank of issue was fully responsible, but in terms of a legal tender money provided by a privileged central bank of issue, which then was in effect under the necessity of supplying the cash needed for the redemption of the notes of the private banks of issue. That would have been a wholly indefensible system which was prevented (at least so

---

[1] A good survey of this discussion will be found in V. C. Smith [55].

[86]

far as the issue of notes, though not the issue of cheque deposits, was concerned) by the prohibition of private note issue.

**

The demands for free banking (i.e. for the free issue of bank notes) were mostly based on the ground that banks would thereby be enabled to provide more and cheaper credit. They were for the same reason resisted by those who recognised that the effect would be inflationary—although at least one advocate of the freedom of note issue had supported it on the ground that

'what is called freedom of banking would result in the total suppression of bank notes in France. I want to give everybody the right to issue bank notes so that nobody should take any bank notes any longer'.[1]

The idea was, of course, that the inevitable abuse of this right, i.e. the issue of an amount of notes which the banks could not redeem from their own reserves, would lead to their failure.

The ultimate victory of the advocates of the centralisation of the national note issue was, however, in effect softened by a concession to those who were mainly interested in the banks being able to provide cheap credit. It consisted in the acknowledgement of a duty of the privileged bank of issue to supply the commercial banks with any notes they needed in order to redeem their demand deposits—rapidly growing in importance. This decision, or rather recognition of a practice into which central banks had drifted, produced a most unfortunate hybrid system in which responsibility for the total quantity of money was divided in a fatal manner so that nobody was in a position to control it effectively.

Demand deposits are like bank notes or cheques

This unfortunate development came about because for a long time it was not generally understood that deposits subject to cheque played very much the same role, and could be created by the commercial banks in exactly the same manner, as bank notes. The consequent dilution of what was still believed to be a government monopoly of the issue of all money resulted in the control of the total circulation of money being divided between a central bank and a large number of commercial

[1] H. Cernuschi [9], as quoted by L. v. Mises [47], p. 446; also V. C. Smith [55], p. 91.

banks whose creation of credit it could influence only indirectly. Not till much later did it come to be understood that the 'inherent instability of credit'[1] under that system was a necessary outcome of this feature; that liquid means was mostly supplied by institutions which themselves had to keep liquid in terms of another form of money, so that they had to *reduce* their outstanding obligations precisely when everybody else also desired to be *more* liquid. By that time this kind of structure had become so firmly established that, in spite of the 'perverse elasticity of the supply of credit'[2] it produced, it came to be regarded as unalterable. Walter Bagehot had clearly seen this dilemma a hundred years ago but despaired of the possibility of remedying this defect of the firmly established banking structure.[3] And Wicksell and later von Mises made it clear that this arrangement must lead to violent recurring fluctuations of business activity—the so-called 'trade-cycle'.

New controls over currencies; new banking practices

Not the least advantage of the proposed abolition of the the government monopoly of the issue of money is that it would provide an opportunity to extricate ourselves from the *impasse* into which this development had led. It would create the conditions in which responsibility for the control of the quantity of the currency is placed on agencies whose self-interest would make them control it in such a manner as to make it most acceptable to the users.

This also shows that the proposed reform requires a complete change in the practices not only of the banks which take up the business of issuing currency but also of those which do not. For the latter could no longer rely on being bailed out by a central bank if they could not meet from their own reserves

---

[1] The expression was originally coined by R. G. Hawtrey.

[2] Cf. L. Currie [12].

[3] W. Bagehot [3], p. 160: 'I have tediously insisted that the natural system of banking is that of many banks keeping their own reserves, with the penalty of failure before them if they neglect it. I have shown that our system is that of a single bank keeping the whole reserve under no effectual penalty of failure. And yet I propose to retain that system and only attempt to mend and palliate it . . . because I am quite sure that it is of no manner of use proposing to alter it . . . there is no force to be found adequate to so vast a reconstruction, and so vast a destruction, and therefore it is useless proposing them.' That was almost certainly true so long as the prevailing system worked tolerably, but not after it had broken down.

their customers' demands for cash—not even if they chose to keep their accounts in terms of the currency issued by a still existing governmental central bank which, to maintain its circulation, would have to adopt the practices of the other issuing banks with which it competed.

Opposition to new system from established bankers . . .

This necessity of all banks to develop wholly new practices will undoubtedly be the cause of strong opposition to the abolition of the government monopoly. It is unlikely that most of the older bankers, brought up in the prevailing routine of banking, will be capable of coping with those problems. I am certain that many of the present leaders of the profession will not be able to conceive how it could possibly work and therefore will describe the whole system as impracticable and impossible.

Especially in countries where competition among banks has for generations been restricted by cartel arrangements, usually tolerated and even encouraged by governments, the older generation of bankers would probably be completely unable even to imagine how the new system would operate and therefore be practically unanimous in rejecting it. But this foreseeable opposition of the established practitioners ought not to deter us. I am also convinced that if a new generation of young bankers were given the opportunity they would rapidly develop techniques to make the new forms of banking not only safe and profitable but also much more beneficial to the whole community than the existing one.

. . . and from banking cranks

Another curious source of opposition, at least once they had discovered that the effects of 'free banking' would be exactly the opposite of those they expected, would be all the numerous cranks who had advocated 'free banking' from inflationist motives.[1] Once the public had an alternative, it would become

[1] The list is very long and, apart from the well-known writers whose works are noted under numbers [13], [22], [44] and [51] in the Bibliography (pp. 136, 137, 139, and 140), the series of studies by Edward Clarence Riegel (1879-1953) published between 1929 and 1944 deserves special mention as an instance of how the results of acute insights and long reflection which seem to have gained the attention of an economist of the rank of Irving Fisher may be completely invalidated by an ignorance of elementary economics. A posthumous volume by Riegel, entitled *Flight from Inflation. The Monetary Alternative*, has been announced by the Hecther Foundation, San Pedro, California.

impossible to induce it to hold cheap money, and the desire to get rid of currency that threatened to depreciate would indeed rapidly turn it into a dwindling money. The inflationists would protest because in the end only very 'hard' money would remain. *Money is the one thing competition would not make cheap, because its attractiveness rests on it preserving its 'dearness'.*

*   *The problem of a 'dear' (stable) money*
A competition the chief merit of which is that it keeps the products of the competitors dear raises various interesting questions. In what will the suppliers compete once they have established somewhat similar reputations and trust for keeping their currencies stable? The profits from the issuing business (which amounts to borrowing at zero interest) will be very large and it does not seem probable that very many firms can succeed in it. For this reason services to the enterprises basing their accounting on a bank's currency would be likely to become the chief weapon of competition, and I should not be surprised if the banks were practically to take over the accounting for their customers.

   Though even very large profits of the successfully established issuers of currency would not be too high a price for a good money, they would inevitably create great political difficulties. Quite apart from the inevitable outcry against the profits of the money monopoly, the real threat to the system would be the cupidity of Ministers of Finance who would soon claim a share in them for the permission to allow a currency to circulate in their country, which would of course spoil everything. It might indeed prove to be nearly as impossible for a democratic government not to interfere with money as to regulate it sensibly.

   The real danger is thus that, while today the people submissively put up with almost any abuse of the money prerogative by government, as soon as it will be possible to say that money is issued by 'rich financial institutions', the complaint about their abuse of the alleged monopoly will become incessant. To wring from the money power their alleged privilege will become the constant demand of demagogues. I trust the banks would be wise enough not to desire even a distant approach to a monopoly position, but to limit the volume of their business may become one of their most delicate problems.

**

[90]

XVII. NO MORE GENERAL INFLATION OR DEFLATION?

Neither a *general* increase nor a *general* decrease of prices appears to be possible in normal circumstances so long as several issuers of different currencies are allowed freely to compete without the interference of government. There will always be one or more issuers who find it to their advantage to regulate the supply of their currency so as to keep its value constant in step with the aggregate price of a bundle of widely used commodities. This would soon force any less provident issuers of competing currencies to put a stop to a slide in the value of their currency in either direction if they did not wish to lose the issue business altogether or to find the value of their currency falling to zero.

No such thing as oil-price (or any other) cost-push inflation

It is, of course, taken for granted here that the average prices in terms of a currency can always be controlled by appropriate adjustments of its quantity. Theoretical analysis and experience seem to me alike to confirm this proposition. We need therefore pay no attention to the views always advanced in periods of prolonged inflation in attempts to exculpate governments by contending that the continued rise in prices is not the fault of policy but the result of an initial rise in costs. To this claim it must be replied emphatically that, in the strict sense, there is simply no such a thing as a 'cost-push' inflation. Neither higher wages nor higher prices of oil, or perhaps of imports generally, can drive up the aggregate price of all goods *unless the purchasers are given more money to buy them*. What is called a cost-push inflation is merely the effect of increases in the quantity of money which governments feel forced to provide in order to prevent the unemployment resulting from a rise in wages (or other costs), which preceded it and which was conceded in the expectation that government would increase the quantity of money. They mean thereby to make it possible for all the workers to find employment through a rise in the demand for their products. If government did not increase the quantity of money such a rise in the wages of a group of workers would not lead to a rise in the general price level but simply to a reduction in sales and therefore to unemployment.

*

It is, however, worth considering a little more fully what would happen if a cartel or other monopolistic organisation, such as a trade union, did succeed in substantially raising the price of an important raw material or the wages of a large group of workers, fixing them in terms of a currency which the issuer endeavours to keep stable. In such circumstances the stability of the price level in terms of this currency could be achieved only by the reduction of a number of other prices. If people have to pay a larger amount of money for the oil or the books and printed papers they consume, they will have to consume less of some other things.

The problem of rigid prices and wages

No currency, of course, can remove the rigidity of some prices which has developed. But it can make impossible the policies which have assisted this development by making it necessary for those who hold prices rigid in the face of a reduced demand to accept the consequent loss of sales.

The whole difference of approach between the dominant 'Keynesian' school and the view underlying the present exposition rests in the last resort on the position taken with regard to the phenomenon of rigid prices and wages. Keynes was largely led to his views by his belief that the increasing rigidity of wages was an unalterable fact which had to be accepted and the effect of which could be mitigated only by accommodating the rate of money expenditure to the given rate of wages. (This opinion was in some measure justified in the British position in the 1920s, when, as a result of an injudicious attempt to raise the external value of the pound, most British wages had become out of line with international commodity prices.) I have maintained ever since that such an adaptation of the quantity of money to the rigidity of some prices and particularly wages would greatly extend the range of such rigidities and must therefore, in the long run, entirely destroy the functioning of the market.

The error of the 'beneficial mild inflation'

All inflation is so very dangerous precisely because many people, including many economists, regard a mild inflation as harmless and even beneficial. But there are few mistakes of policy with regard to which it is more important to heed the old maxim *principiis obsta*.[1] Apparently, and surprisingly, the self-accelerating mechanism of all engineered inflation is not yet understood even by some economists. The initial general stimulus which an increase of the quantity of money provides is chiefly due to the fact that prices and therefore profits turn out to be higher than expected. Every venture succeeds, including even some which ought to fail. But this can last only so long as the continuous rise of prices is not generally expected. Once people learn to count on it, even a continued rise of prices at the same rate will no longer exert the stimulus that it gave at first.

Monetary policy is then faced with an unpleasant dilemma. In order to maintain the degree of activity it created by mild inflation, it will have to accelerate the rate of inflation, and will have to do so again and again at an ever increasing rate every time the prevailing rate of inflation comes to be expected. If it fails to do so and either stops accelerating or ceases to inflate altogether, the economy will be in a much worse position than when the process started. Not only has inflation allowed the ordinary errors of judgement to accumulate which are normally promptly eliminated and will now all have to be liquidated at the same time. It will in addition have caused misdirection of production and drawn labour and other resources into activities which could be maintained only if the additional investment financed by the increase in the quantity of money could be maintained.

Since it has become generally understood that whoever controls the total supply of money of a country has thereby power to give in most situations almost instantaneous relief to unemployment, even if only at the price of much unemployment later, the political pressure on such an agency must become irresistible. The threat of that possibility has always been understood by some economists, who for this reason have ever been anxious to restrain the monetary authorities by barriers they could not break. But since the betrayal, or ignorance, of this insight by a school of theorists which thereby bought themselves temporary popularity, political control of the supply of money has become too dangerous to the preservation of the market order to be any longer tolerated. However

[1] ['Resist beginnings' (or, colloquially, 'nip it in the bud'): Ovid, *Remedia Amoris*, 91, trans. Showerman, *Oxford Dictionary of Quotations*, OUP. – ED.]

much political pressure might be brought on the most important private banks of issue to make them relax their credit conditions and extend their circulation, if a *non-monopolistic* institution gave in to such pressure it would soon cease to be one of the most important issuers.

The 'money illusion', i.e. the belief that money represents a constant value, could arise only because it was useless to worry about changes in the value of money so long as one could not do anything about it. Once people have a choice they will become very much aware of the different changes of the value of the different currencies accessible to them. It would, as it should, become common knowledge that money needs to be watched, and would be regarded as a praiseworthy action rather than as an unpatriotic deed to warn people that a particular currency was suspect.

**

Responsibility for unemployment would be traced back to trade unions

Depriving government of the power of thus counteracting the effects of monopolistically enforced increases in wages or prices by increasing the quantity of money would place the responsibility for the full use of resources back to where it belongs: where the causally effective decisions are taken—the monopolists who negotiate the wages or prices. We ought to understand by now that the attempt to combat by inflation the unemployment caused by the monopolistic actions of trade unions will merely postpone the effects on employment to the time when the rate of inflation required to maintain employment by continually increasing the quantity of money becomes unbearable. The sooner we can make impossible such harmful measures, probably unavoidable so long as government has the monetary power to take them, the better for all concerned.

The scheme proposed here would, indeed, do somewhat more than prevent only inflations and deflations in the strict sense of these terms. Not all changes in the general level of prices are caused by changes in the quantity of money, or its failure to adapt itself to changes in the demand for holding money; and only those brought about in this manner can properly be called inflation or deflation. It is true that there are nowadays unlikely to be large simultaneous changes in the supply of many of the most important goods, as happened when variations in harvests could cause dearths or gluts of most of the main foodstuffs and clothing materials. And, even today, perhaps in wartime in a country surrounded by enemies or on an island, an acute scarcity (or glut) of the products in which the country has specialised is perhaps conceivable. At least if the index number of commodity prices that guided the issue of the currency in the country were based chiefly on national prices, such a rule might lead to changes in the supply of currency designed to counteract price movements not caused by monetary factors.

Preventing general deflation

The reader may not yet feel fully reassured that, in the kind of competitive money system we are here contemplating, a general deflation will be as impossible as a general inflation. Experience seems indeed to have shown that, in conditions of severe uncertainty or alarm about the future, even very low rates of interest cannot prevent a shrinking of a bank's outstanding loans. What could a bank issuing its own distinct currency do when it finds itself in such a situation, and commodity prices in terms of its currency threaten to fall? And how strong would be its interest in stopping such a fall of prices if the same circumstances affected the competing institutions in the same way?

There would of course be no difficulty in placing additional money at a time when people in general want to keep very liquid. The issuing bank, on the other hand, would not wish to incur an obligation to maintain by redemption a value of its currency higher than that at which it had issued it. To maintain profitable investments, the bank would presumably be driven to buy interest-bearing securities and thereby put cash into the hands of people looking for other investments as well as bring down the long-term rates of interest, with a similar effect. An institution with a very large circulation of currency might even find it expedient to buy for storage quantities of commodities represented in the index that tended to fall particularly strongly in price.

This would probably be sufficient to counteract any downward tendency of general prices produced by the economic process itself, and if it achieved this effect it is probably as much as can be accomplished by any management of money. But it is of course not to be wholly excluded that some events may cause such a general state of discouragement and lethargy that nothing could induce people to resume investment and

[95]

thereby stop an impending fall of prices. So far as this were due to extraneous events, such as the fear of an impending world catastrophe or of the imminent advent of communism, or in some region the desire to convert all private possessions into cash to be prepared for flight, probably nothing could prevent a general fall in the prices of possessions that are not easily portable. But so long as the general conditions for the effective conduct of capitalist enterprise persisted, competition would provide a money that caused as little disturbance to its working as possible. And this is probably all we can hope.[1]

XVIII. MONETARY POLICY NEITHER DESIRABLE NOR POSSIBLE

It is true that under the proposed arrangements monetary policy as we now know it could not exist. It is not to be denied that, with the existing sort of division of responsibility between the issues of the basic money and those of a parasitic circulation based on it, central banks must, to prevent matters from getting completely out of hand, try deliberately to forestall developments they can only influence but not directly control. But the central banking system, which only 50 years ago was regarded as the crowning achievement of financial wisdom, has largely discredited itself. This is even more true since, with the abandonment of the gold standard and fixed exchange rates, the central banks have acquired fuller discretionary powers than when they were still trying to act on firm rules. And this is true no less where the aim of policy is still a reasonable degree of stability, as in countries overwhelmed by inflation.

Government the major source of instability

We have it on the testimony of a competent authority who was by no means unsympathetic to those modern aspirations that, during the recent decade 1962 to 1972 when the believers in a 'fine tuning' of monetary policy had an influence which we must hope they will never have again, the larger part of the

---

[1] The remaining doubt concerns the question whether in such circumstances the holders of cash might wish to switch towards an appreciating currency, but such a currency would then probably not be available.

fluctuations were a consequence of budgetary and monetary policy.[1] And it is certainly impossible to claim that the period since the abandonment of the semi-automatic regulation of the quantity of money has *generally* been more stable or free from monetary disturbances than the periods of the gold standard or fixed rates of exchange.

We indeed begin to see how completely different an economic landscape the free issue of competitive currencies would produce when we realise that under such a system what is known today as monetary policy would neither be needed nor even possible. The issuing banks, guided solely by their striving for gain, would thereby serve the public interest better than any institution has ever done or could do that supposedly aimed at it. There neither would exist a definable quantity of money of a nation or region, nor would it be desirable that the individual issuers of the several currencies should aim at anything but to make as large as possible the aggregate value of their currency that the public was prepared to hold at the given value of the unit. If we are right that, being able to choose, the public would prefer a currency whose purchasing power it could expect to be stable, this would provide a better currency and secure more stable business conditions than have ever existed before.

The supposed chief weakness of the market order, the recurrence of periods of mass unemployment, is always pointed out by socialists and other critics as an inseparable and unpardonable defect of capitalism.[2] It proves in fact wholly to be the result of government preventing private enterprise from working freely and providing itself with a money that would secure stability. We have seen that there can be no doubt that free enterprise would have been both able to provide a money securing stability and that striving for individual gain would have driven private financial institutions to do so if they

---

[1] O. Eckstein [14], especially p. 19: 'Traditionally, stabilisation theory has viewed private, capitalist economy as a mechanism which produces fluctuations. ...There is no question that government is a major source of instability.' And p. 25: 'The rate of inflation [in the US between 1962 and 1972] would have been substantially less, real growth would have been smoother, the total amount of unemployment experienced would have been little changed but the variations would have been milder, and the terminal conditions at the end of the period would have made it possible to avoid the wage and price controls.'

[2] The long depression of the 1930s, which led to the revival of Marxism (which would probably have been dead today without it), was wholly due to the mismanagement of money by government—before as well as after the crisis of 1929.

had been permitted. I am not sure that private enterprise would adopt the manner of performing the task I have suggested, but I am inclined to think that, by its habitual procedure of selecting the most successful, it would in time throw up better solutions to these problems than anyone can foresee today.

Monetary policy a cause of depressions

What we should have learned is that monetary policy is much more likely to be a cause than a cure of depressions, because it is much easier, by giving in to the clamour for cheap money, to cause those misdirections of production that make a later reaction inevitable, than to assist the economy in extricating itself from the consequences of overdeveloping in particular directions. *The past instability of the market economy is the consequence of the exclusion of the most important regulator of the market mechanism, money, from itself being regulated by the market process.*

A single monopolistic governmental agency can neither possess the information which should govern the supply of money nor would it, if it knew what it ought to do in the general interest, usually be in a position to act in that manner. Indeed, if, as I am convinced, the main advantage of the market order is that prices will convey to the acting individuals the relevant information, only the constant observation of the course of current prices of particular commodities can provide information on the direction in which more or less money ought to be spent. Money is not a tool of policy that can achieve particular foreseeable results by control of its quantity. But it should be part of the self-steering mechanism by which individuals are constantly induced to adjust their activities to circumstances on which they have information only through the abstract signals of prices. It should be a serviceable link in the process that communicates the effects of events never wholly known to anybody and that is required to maintain an order in which the plans of participating persons match.

Government cannot act in the general interest

Yet even if we assumed that government could know what should be done about the supply of money in the general interest, it is highly unlikely that it would be able to act in that manner. As Professor Eckstein, in the article quoted above, concludes from his experience in advising governments:

'Governments are not able to live by the rules even if they were to adopt the philosophy [of providing a stable framework]'.[1]

Once governments are given the power to benefit particular groups or sections of the population, the mechanism of majority government forces them to use it to gain the support of a sufficient number of them to command a majority. The constant temptation to meet local or sectional dissatisfaction by manipulating the quantity of money so that more can be spent on services for those clamouring for assistance will often be irresistible. Such expenditure is not an appropriate remedy but necessarily upsets the proper functioning of the market.

In a true emergency such as war, governments would of course still be able to force upon people bonds or other pieces of paper for unavoidable payments which cannot be made from current revenues. Compulsory loans and the like would probably be more compatible with the required rapid readjustments of industry to radically changed circumstances than an inflation that suspends the effective working of the price mechanism.

*

No more balance-of-payment problems

With the disappearance of distinct territorial currencies there would of course also disappear the so-called 'balance-of-payment problems' believed to cause intense difficulties to present-day monetary policy. There would, necessarily, be continuous redistributions of the relative and absolute quantities of currency in different regions as some grew relatively richer and others relatively poorer. But this would create no more difficulties than the same process causes today within any large country. People who grew richer would have more money and those who grew poorer would have less. That would be all. The special difficulties caused by the fact that under existing arrangements the reduction of the distinct cash basis of one country requires a contraction of the whole separate superstructure of credit erected on it would no longer exist.

Similarly, the closer connections of the structure of the prices

[1] O. Eckstein [14], p. 26.

prevailing within any one country as against prices in neighbouring countries, and with it the statistical illusion of the relative movement of distinct national price levels, would largely disappear. Indeed it would be discovered that 'balance-of-payment problems' are a quite unnecessary effect of the existence of distinct national currencies, which is the cause of the wholly undesirable closer coherence of national prices than of international prices. From the angle of a desirable international economic order the 'balance-of-payment problem' is a pseudo-problem about which nobody need worry but a monopolist of the issue of money for a given territory. And not the least advantage of the disappearance of distinct national currencies would be that we could return to the happy days of statistical innocence in which nobody could know what the balance of payment of his country or region was and thus nobody could worry or would have to care about it.

The addictive drug of cheap money

The belief that cheap money is always desirable and beneficial makes inevitable and irresistible the pressure on any political authority or monopolist known to be capable of making money cheap by issuing more of it. Yet loanable funds made artificially cheap by creating more money for lending them, not only help those to whom they are lent, though at the expense of others, but for a while have a general stimulating effect on business activity. That at the same time such issues have the effect of destroying the steering mechanism of the market is not so easily seen. But supplies of such funds for additional purchases of goods produce a distortion of the structure of relative prices which draws resources into activities that cannot be lastingly maintained and thereby become the cause of an inevitable later reaction. These indirect and slow effects are, however, in their nature very much more difficult to recognise or understand than the immediate pleasant effects and particularly the benefits to those to whom the additional money goes in the first instance.

To provide a medium of exchange for people who want to hold it until they wish to buy an equivalent for what they have supplied to others is a useful service like producing any other good. If an increase in the demand for such cash balances is met by an increase of the quantity of money (or a reduction of the balances people want to hold by a corresponding decrease of the total amount of money), it does not disturb the correspondence between demand and supply of all other commodities or services. But it is really a crime like theft to enable some people to buy more than they have earned by more than the amount which other people have at the same time foregone to claim.

When committed by a monopolistic issuer of money, and especially by government, it is however a very lucrative crime which is generally tolerated and remains unpunished because its consequences are not understood. But for the issuer of a currency which has to compete with other currencies, it would be a suicidal act, because it would destroy the service for which people did want to hold his currency.

Because of a lack of general understanding, the crime of over-issue by a monopolist is still not only tolerated but even applauded. That is one of the chief reasons why the smooth working of the market is so frequently upset. But today almost any statesman who tries to do good in this field, and certainly anyone forced to do what the large organised interests think good, is therefore likely to do much more harm than good. On the other hand, anyone who merely knows that the success of his business of issuing money rests wholly on his ability to keep the buying power of his currency constant, will do more for the public good by aiming solely at large profits for himself than by any conscious concern about the more remote effects of his actions.

The abolition of central banks

Perhaps a word should be explicitly inserted here about the obvious corollary that the abolition of the government monopoly of the issue of money should involve also the disappearance of central banks as we know them, both because one might conceive of some private bank assuming the function of a central bank and because it might be thought that, even without a government monopoly of issue, some of the classic functions of central banks, such as that of acting as 'lender of last resort' or of 'holder of the ultimate reserve',[1] might still be required.

The need for such an institution is, however, entirely due to the commercial banks incurring liabilities payable on demand

---

[1] The standard description of this function and of how it arose is still W. Bagehot, who could rightly speak [3, p. 142] of 'a natural state of banking, that in which all the principal banks kept their own reserve'.

in a unit of currency which some other bank has the sole right to issue, thus in effect creating money redeemable in terms of another money. This, as we shall have still to consider, is indeed the chief cause of the instability of the existing credit system, and through it of the wide fluctuations in all economic activity. Without the central bank's (or the government's) monopoly of issuing money, and the legal tender provisions of the law, there would be no justification whatever for the banks to rely for their solvency on the cash to be provided by another body. The 'one reserve system', as Walter Bagehot called it, is an inseparable accompaniment of the monopoly of issue but unnecessary and undesirable without it.

It might still be argued that central banks are necessary to secure the required 'elasticity' of the circulation. And though this expression has probably in the past been more abused than any other to disguise inflationist demands, we must not overlook its valid kernel. The manner in which elasticity of supply and stability of value of the money can be reconciled is a genuine problem, and it will be solved only if the issuer of a given currency is aware that his business depends on so regulating the quantity of his currency that the value of its unit remains stable (in terms of commodities). If an addition to the quantity would lead to a rise of prices, it would clearly not be justified, however urgently some may feel that they need additional cash—which then will be cash to spend and not to add to their liquidity reserves. What makes a currency a universally acceptable, that is really liquid, asset will be precisely that it is preferred to other assets because its buying power is expected to remain constant.

What is necessarily scarce is not liquidity but buying power—the command over goods for consumption or use in further production, and this is limited because there is no more than a given amount of these things to buy. So far as people want more liquid assets solely to hold them but not to spend them, they can be manufactured without thereby depreciating their value. But if people want more liquid assets in order to spend them on goods, the value of such credits will melt between their fingers.

No fixing of rates of interest

With the central banks and the monopoly of the issue of money would, of course, disappear also the possibility of deliberately determining the rate of interest. The disappearance of what is called 'interest policy' is wholly desirable. The rate of interest, like any other price, ought to record the aggregate effects of thousands of circumstances affecting the demand for and supply of loans which cannot possibly be known to any one agency. The effects of most price changes are unpleasant to some, and, like other price changes, changes in the rate of interest convey to all concerned that an aggregate of circumstances which nobody knows has made them necessary. The whole idea that the rate of interest ought to be used as an instrument of policy is entirely mistaken, since only competition in a free market can take account of all the circumstances which ought to be taken account of in the determination of the rate of interest.

So long as each separate issue bank in its lending activity aimed at regulating the volume of its outstanding currency so as to keep its buying power constant, the rate of interest at which it could do so would be determined for it by the market. And, on the whole, the lending for investment purposes of all the banks together, if it was not to drive up the price level, could not exceed the current volume of savings (and conversely, if it was not to depress the price level, must not fall short of the current volume of savings) by more than was required to increase aggregate demand in step with a growing volume of output. The rate of interest would then be determined by balancing the demand for money for spending purposes with the supply required for keeping the price level constant. I believe this would assure as close an agreement between saving and investment as we can hope to achieve, leaving a balance of change in the quantity of money to take account of changes in the demand for money caused by changes in the balances people want to hold.

Of course, government would still affect this market rate of interest by the net volume of its borrowing. But it could no longer practise those most pernicious manipulations of the rate of interest which are intended to enable it to borrow cheaply— a practice which has done so much harm in the past that this effect alone would seem an adequate reason why government should be kept away from the tap.

**

XIX. A BETTER DISCIPLINE THAN FIXED RATES OF EXCHANGE

Readers who know of my consistent support over more than 40 years of fixed rates of exchange between national currencies, and of my critique of a system of flexible rates of foreign exchange,[1] even after most of my fellow defenders of a free market had become converts to this system, will probably feel at first that my present position is in conflict with, or even represents a complete reversal of, my former views. This is not so. In two respects my present proposal is a result of the further development of the considerations which determined my former position.

In the first instance, I have always regarded it as thoroughly undesirable that the structure of the prices of commodities and services in one country should be lifted and lowered as a whole relatively to the price structure of other countries in order to correct some alteration in the supply of or demand for a particular commodity. This was erroneously thought to be necessary chiefly because the availability of statistical information in the form of index numbers of the *average* movement of prices in one country gave the misleading impression that 'the internal value' of one currency as such had to be changed relatively to the value of other currencies, while what was required were primarily changes of the relations between particular prices in all the countries concerned. So far as the assumed necessity of changes in relation between general prices in the countries was true, this was an artificial and undesirable effect of the imperfection of the international monetary system which the gold standard with a superstructure of deposit money produced. We will consider these questions further in the next section.

Remove protection of official currency from competition

Secondly, I had regarded fixed rates of exchange as necessary for the same reason for which I now plead for completely free

<hr>

[1] The first systematic exposition of my position will be found in my 1937 Geneva lectures on *Monetary Nationalism and International Stability* [27]. It contains a series of lectures hastily and badly written on a topic to which I had earlier committed myself but which I had to write when I was pre-occupied with other problems. I still believe that it contains important arguments against flexible exchange rates between national currencies which have never been adequately answered, but I am not surprised that few people appear ever to have read it.

markets for all kinds of currency, namely that it was required to impose a very necessary discipline or restraint on the agencies issuing money. Neither I, nor apparently anybody else, then thought of the much more effective discipline that would operate if the providers of money were deprived of the power of shielding the money they issued against the rivalry of *competing currencies*.

The compulsion to maintain a fixed rate of redemption in terms of gold or other currencies has in the past provided the only discipline that effectively prevented monetary authorities from giving in to the demands of the ever-present pressure for cheap money. The gold standard, fixed rates of exchange, or any other form of obligatory conversion at a fixed rate, served no other purpose than to impose upon the issuers of money such a discipline and, by making its regulation automatic, to deprive them of the power arbitrarily to change the quantity of money. It is a discipline that has proved too weak to prevent governments from breaking it. Yet, though the regulations achieved by those automatic controls were far from ideal or even tolerably satisfactory, so long as currencies were thus regulated they were much more satisfactory than anything the discretionary powers of governmental monopolies have ever achieved for any length of time. Nothing short of the belief that it would be a national disgrace for a country not to live up to its obligations has ever sufficed adequately to strengthen the resistance of monetary authorities against pressures for cheap money. I should never have wanted to deny that a very wise and politically independent monetary authority might do better than it is compelled to do in order to preserve a fixed parity with gold or another currency. But I can see no hope of monetary authorities in the real world prevailing for any length of time in their good intentions.

Better even than gold—the 'wobbly anchor'

It ought by now of course to be generally understood that the value of a currency redeemable in gold (or in another currency) is not *derived* from the value of that gold, but merely kept at the same value through the automatic regulation of its quantity. The superstition dies only slowly, but even under a gold standard it is no more (or perhaps even less) true that the value of the currency is determined by the value in other uses of the gold it contains (or by its costs of production) than is

[105]

the converse, that the value of gold is determined by the value of the currencies into which it can be converted. Historically it is true that all the money that preserved its value for any length of time was metallic (or money convertible into metal—gold or silver); and governments sooner or later used to debase even metallic money, so that all the kinds of paper money of which we have experience were so much worse. Most people therefore now believe that relief can come only from returning to a metallic (or other commodity) standard. But not only is a metallic money also exposed to the risks of fraud by government; even at its best it would never be as good a money as one issued by an agency whose whole business rested on its success in providing a money the public preferred to other kinds. Though gold is an anchor—and any anchor is better than a money left to the discretion of government—it is a very wobbly anchor. It certainly could not bear the strain if the majority of countries tried to run their own gold standard. There just is not enough gold about. An international gold standard could today mean only that a few countries maintained a real gold standard while the others hung on to them through a gold exchange standard.

Competition would provide better money than would government

I believe we can do much better than gold ever made possible. Governments cannot do better. Free enterprise, i.e. the institutions that would emerge from a process of competition in providing good money, no doubt would. There would in that event also be no need to encumber the money supply with the complicated and expensive provision for convertibility which was necessary to secure the automatic operation of the gold standard and which made it appear as at least more practicable than what would ideally seem much more suitable—a commodity reserve standard. A very attractive scheme for storing a large variety of raw materials and other standard commodities had been worked out for such a standard to ensure the redeemability of the currency unit by a fixed combination of such commodities and thereby the stability of the currency. Storage would however be so expensive, and practicable only for such a small collection of commodities, as to reduce the value of the proposal.[1] But some such pre-

[1] Cf. Friedman [19].

[106]

caution to force the issuer to regulate the amount of his currency appears necessary or desirable only so long as his interest would be to increase or decrease its value above or below the standard. Convertibility is a safeguard necessary to impose upon a *monopolist*, but unnecessary with *competing* suppliers who cannot maintain themselves in the business unless they provide money at least as advantageous to the user as anybody else.

Government monopoly of money unnecessary

Not so very long ago, in 1960, I myself argued that it is not only impracticable but probably undesirable even if possible to deprive governments of their control over monetary policy.[1] This view was still based on the common tacit assumption that there must be in each country a single uniform kind of money. I did not then even consider the possibility of true competition between currencies within any given country or region. If only one kind of money is permitted, it is probably true that the monopoly of its issue must be under the control of government. The concurrent circulation of several currencies might at times be slightly inconvenient, but careful analysis of its effects indicates that the advantages appear to be so very much greater than the inconveniences that they hardly count in comparison, though unfamiliarity with the new situation makes them appear much bigger than they probably would be.

Difference between voluntarily accepted and enforced paper money

Much as all historical experience appears to justify the deep mistrust most people harbour against paper money, it is well founded only with regard to money issued by *government*. Frequently the term 'fiat money' is used as if it applied to all paper money, but the expression refers of course only to money which has been given currency by the arbitrary decree or other act of authority. Money which is current only because people have been forced to accept it is wholly different from money that has come to be accepted because people trust the issuer to keep it stable. Voluntarily accepted paper money therefore ought not to suffer from the evil reputation governments have given paper money.

[1] Hayek [29], pp. 324 *et seq.*

Money is valued because, and in so far as, it is known to be scarce, and is for this reason likely to be accepted at the going value by others. And any money which is voluntarily used only because it is trusted to be kept scarce by the issuer, and which will be held by people only so long as the issuer justifies that trust, will increasingly confirm its acceptability at the established value. People will know that the risk they run in holding it will be smaller than the risk they run in holding any other good on which they do not possess special information. Their willingness to hold it will rest on the experience that other people will be ready to accept it at an approximately known range of prices because they also have learnt to hold the same expectation, and so on. This is a state of affairs that can continue indefinitely and will even tend to stabilise itself more and more as confirmed expectations increase the trust.

*

Some people apparently find it difficult to believe that a mere token money which did not give the holder a legal claim for redemption in terms of some object possessing an intrinsic value (equal to its current value) could ever be generally accepted for any length of time or preserve its value. They seem to forget that for the past 40 years in the whole Western World there has been no other money than such irredeemable tokens. The various paper currencies we have had to use have preserved a value which for some time was only slowly decreasing not because of any hope of ultimate redemption, but only because the monopolistic agencies authorised to issue the exclusive kind of currency of a particular country did in some inadequate degree restrict its amount. But the clause on a pound-note saying 'I promise to pay to the bearer on demand the sum of one pound', or whatever the figure be, signed for the Governor and Company of the Bank of England by their Chief Cashier, means of course no more than that they promise to exchange that piece of paper for other pieces of paper.

It is entirely at the discretion of these institutions or governments to regulate the total amount of their issues in circulation by exchanging some of the notes for other kinds of money or for securities. This sort of redemption is just a method of regulating the quantity of money in the hands of the public, and, so long as public opinion was not misguided by specious theories, it has always been taken as a matter of course that, e.g., 'the value of [greenbacks] changes as the government chooses to enlarge or to contract the issue'.[1]

History certainly disproves the suggestion that in this respect government, which only profits from excessive issues, can be trusted more than a private issuer whose whole business depends on his not abusing that trust. Does anyone really believe that in the industrial countries of the West, after the experience of the last half-century, anybody trusts the value of government-sponsored money more than he would trust money issued by a private agency whose business was understood to depend wholly on its issuing good money?

**

XX. SHOULD THERE BE SEPARATE CURRENCY AREAS?

We are so used to the existence in each country of a distinct currency in which practically all internal transactions are conducted that we tend to regard it also as natural and necessary for the whole structure of internal prices to move together relatively to the price structure of other countries. This is by no means a necessary or in any sense natural or desirable state of affairs.

National currencies not inevitable or desirable

At least without tariffs or other obstructions to the free movement of goods and men across frontiers, the tendency of national prices to move in unison is an *effect* of, rather than a justification for, maintaining separate national currency systems. And it has led to the growth of national institutions, such as nation-wide collective bargaining, which have intensified these differences. The reason for this development is that the control over the supply of money gives national governments more power over actions which are wholly undesirable from the point of view of international order and stability. It is the kind of arrangement of which only *étatists* of various complexions can approve but which is wholly inimical to frictionless international relations.

There is indeed little reason why, apart from the effects of

[1] W. Bagehot [3], p. 12.

monopolies made possible by national protection, territories that happen to be under the same government should form distinct national economic areas which would benefit by having a common currency distinct from that of other areas. In an order largely dependent on international exchange, it was rather absurd to treat the often accidental agglomeration of different regions under the same government as a distinct economic area. The recognition of this truth has however only recently led a few economists to ask what would be desirable currency areas—a question they found rather difficult to answer.[1]

While historically distinct national currencies were simply an instrument to enhance the power of national governments, the modern argument for monetary nationalism favours an arrangement under which *all* prices in a region can simultaneously be raised or lowered *relatively* to *all* prices in other regions. This is regarded as an advantage because it avoids the necessity to lower a group of particular prices, especially wages, when foreign demand for the products concerned has fallen and shifted to some other national region. But it is a political makeshift; in practice it means that, instead of lowering the *few* prices immediately affected, a very much *larger* number of prices will have to be raised to restore international equilibrium after the international price of the local currency has been reduced. The original motive for the agitation for flexible rates of exchange between national currencies was therefore purely inflationist, although a foolish attempt was made to place the burden of adjustment on the surplus countries. But it was later also taken up in countries which wanted to protect themselves against the effects of the inflationist policies of others.

*

There is no better case for preventing the decrease of the quantity of money circulating in a region or sector of a larger community than there is for governmental measures to prevent a decrease of the money incomes of particular individuals or groups—even though such measures might temporarily relieve the hardships of the groups living there. It is even essential for honest government that nobody should have the power of relieving groups from the necessity of having to adapt them-

[1] McKinnon [40] and Mundell [49].

selves to unforeseen changes, because, if government can do so, it will be forced by political necessity to do so all the time.

**

Rigidity of wage-rates: raising national price structure is no solution

Experience has shown that what was believed to be the easy way out from the difficulties created by the rigidity of wages, namely, raising the *whole* national price level, is merely making matters worse, since in effect it relieves trade unions of the responsibility for the unemployment their wage demands would otherwise cause and creates an irresistible pressure on governments to mitigate these effects by inflation. I remain therefore as opposed to monetary nationalism[1] or flexible rates of exchange between national currencies as ever. But I prefer now abolishing monetary frontiers altogether to merely making national currencies convertible into each other at a fixed rate. The whole conception of cutting out a particular sector from the international structure of prices and lifting or lowering it, as it were, bodily against all the other prices of the same commodities still seems to me an idea that could be conceived only in the brains of men who have come to think exclusively in terms of national ('macro') price levels, not of individual ('micro') prices. They seem to have thought of national price levels as the acting determinants of human action and to have ceased to understand the function of relative prices.

Stable national price level could disrupt economic activity

There is really no reason why we should want the price level of a region interconnected by a large number of commodity streams with the rest of the world economy to have a stable price level. To keep this price level stable in spite of shifts of demand towards or away from the region only disturbs and does not assist the functioning of the market. The relation between regions or localities is in this respect not essentially different from the relations between countries. The transfer of demand for airplanes from Seattle to Los Angeles will indeed lead to a loss of jobs and a decline of incomes and probably of

[1] The historical origin of the preoccupation with national price levels as well as the other aspects of *Monetary Nationalism* were discussed in my book with that title [27], especially p. 43.

retail prices in Seattle; and if there is a fall in wages in Seattle, it will probably attract other industries. But nothing would be gained, except perhaps for the moment, by increasing the quantity of money in Seattle or the State of Washington. And it would not ease the problem if the whole North West of the United States had a currency of its own which it could keep constant or even increase to meet such a misfortune for some of its inhabitants.

But while we have no foundations for desiring particular areas to have their individual currencies, it is of course an altogether different question whether the free issue of competitive currencies in each area would lead to the formation of currency areas—or rather of areas where different currencies were predominant, although others could be used. As we have seen (Section XII), there might develop different preferences as regard the commodity equivalent of the currency that should be kept constant. In a primitive country where people used little but rice, fish, pork, cotton and timber, they would be chiefly concerned about different prices—though local tendencies of this sort would probably be offset by those of the users to be guided in their preferences by the greater trust they had in an internationally-reputed issuer of money than in one who adapted his currency specially to local circumstances. Nor would I be surprised to find that in large areas only one currency was generally used in ordinary dealings, so long as potential competition made its issuer keep it stable. As everywhere else, so long as it does not come to trying out innovations or improvements, competition *in posse*[1] is likely to be nearly as effective as competition *in esse*.[1] And the ready convertibility of the generally used currency would make all those who had any traffic beyond the region change their holdings quickly enough into another currency if their suspicions about the commonly accepted one were aroused.

Such areas in which one currency predominates would however not have sharp or fixed boundaries but would largely overlap, and their dividing lines would fluctuate. But once the principle were generally accepted in the economically leading countries, it would probably spread rapidly to wherever people could choose their institutions. No doubt there would remain enclaves under dictators who did not wish to

[1] [*In posse*: potential; *in esse*: in being.—ED.]

[112]

let go their power over money—even after the absence of exchange control had become the mark of a civilised and honest country.

XXI. THE EFFECTS ON GOVERNMENT FINANCE AND EXPENDITURE

The two goals of public finance and of the regulation of a satisfactory currency are entirely different from, and largely in conflict with, each other. To place both tasks in the hands of the same agency has in consequence always led to confusion and in recent years has had disastrous consequences. It has not only made money the chief cause of economic fluctuations but has also greatly facilitated an uncontrollable growth of public expenditure. If we are to preserve a functioning market economy (and with it individual freedom), *nothing can be more urgent than that we dissolve the unholy marriage between monetary and fiscal policy*, long clandestine but formally consecrated with the victory of 'Keynesian' economics.

We need not say much more about the unfortunate effects of the 'needs' of finance on the supply of money. Not only have all major inflations until recently been the result of governments covering their financial 'needs' by the printing press. Even during relatively stable periods the regular necessity for central banks to accommodate the financial 'needs' of government by keeping interest rates low has been a constant embarrassment: it has interfered with the banks' efforts to secure stability and has given their policies an inflationist bias that was usually checked only belatedly by the mechanism of the gold standard.

Good national money impossible under democratic government dependent on special interests

I do not think it an exaggeration to say that it is wholly impossible for a central bank subject to political control, or even exposed to serious political pressure, to regulate the quantity of money in a way conducive to a smoothly functioning market order. A good money, like good law, must operate without regard to the effects that decisions of the issuer will have on known groups or individuals. A benevolent dictator

[113]

might conceivably disregard these effects; no democratic government dependent on a number of special interests can possibly do so. But to use the control of the supply of money as an instrument for achieving particular ends destroys the equilibrating operation of the price mechanism, which is required to maintain the continuing process of ordering the market that gives individuals a good chance of having their expectations fulfilled.

Government monopoly of money and government expenditure

But we have probably said enough about the harm that monetary policy guided by financial considerations is likely to do. What we must still consider is the effect that power over the supply of money has had on financial policy. Just as the absence of competition has prevented the monopolist supplier of money from being subject to a salutary discipline, the power over money has also relieved governments of the necessity to keep their expenditure within their revenue. It is largely for this reason that 'Keynesian' economics has become so rapidly popular among socialist economists. Indeed, since ministers of finance were told by economists that running a deficit was a meritorious act, and even that, so long as there were unemployed resources, extra government expenditure cost the people nothing, any effective bar to a rapid increase in government expenditure was destroyed.

There can be little doubt that the spectacular increase in government expenditure over the last 30 years, with governments in some Western countries claiming up to half or more of the national income for collective purposes, was made possible by government control of the issue of money. On the one hand, inflation has constantly pushed people with a given real income into much higher tax brackets than they anticipated when they approved the rates, and thus raised government revenue more rapidly than they had intended. On the other, the habitual large deficits, and the comparative ease with which budgeted figures could be exceeded, still further increased the share of the real output governments were able to claim for their purposes.

Government money and unbalanced budgets

In a sense it is arbitrary to require governments to balance their budget for the calendar year. But the alternations of the seasons and the firmly established business practices of accounting provide a good reason; and the practice of business, where receipts and expenditure are regularly balanced over a period with known fluctuations, further supports the usage. If major economic fluctuations can be prevented by other arrangements, the conventional annual budget is still the best term for requiring such balancing. Assuming it to be true that the regulation of the supply of money by competition between private currencies would secure not only a stable value of money but also stable business conditions, the argument that government deficits are necessary to reduce unemployment amounts to the contention that a government control of money is needed to cure what it is itself causing. There is no reason why, with a stable money, it should ever be desirable to allow government to spend more than it has. And it is certainly more important that government expenditure does not become a cause of general instability than that the clumsy apparatus of government should (in the most unlikely event that it acts in time) be available to mitigate any slackening of economic activity.

The ease with which a minister of finance can today both budget for an excess of expenditure over revenue and exceed that expenditure has created a wholly new style of finance compared with the careful housekeeping of the past. And since the ease with which one demand after another is conceded evokes ever new expectations of further bounty, the process is a self-accelerating one which even men who genuinely wish to avoid it find it impossible to stop. Anyone who knows the difficulty of restraining a bureaucratic apparatus not controlled by profit-and-loss calculations from constantly expanding also knows that without the rigid barrier of strictly limited funds there is nothing to stop an indefinite growth of government expenditure.

Unless we restore a situation in which governments (and other public authorities) find that if they overspend they will, like everybody else, be unable to meet their obligations, there will be no halt to this growth which, by substituting collective for private activity, threatens to suffocate individual initiative. Under the prevailing form of unlimited democracy, in which government has power to confer special material benefits on groups, it is forced to buy the support of sufficient numbers to add up to a majority. Even with the best will in the world, no government can resist this pressure unless it can point to a firm barrier it cannot cross. While governments will of course occasionally be forced to borrow from the public to meet unforeseen requirements, or choose to finance some investments in that manner, it is highly undesirable in any circumstances that these funds should be provided by the creation of additional money. Nor is it desirable that those additions to the total quantity of money which are required in a growing economy to equip the suppliers of additional factors of production with the needed cash balances should be introduced into circulation in this manner.

Government power over money facilitates centralisation

There can be little doubt also that the ability of central governments to resort to this kind of finance is one of the contributory causes of the advance in the most undesirable centralisation of government. Nothing can be more welcome than depriving government of its power over money and so stopping the apparently irresistible trend towards an accelerating increase of the share of the national income it is able to claim. If allowed to continue, this trend would in a few years bring us to a state in which governments would claim 100 per cent (in Sweden and Britain it already exceeds 60 per cent) of all resources—and would in consequence become literally 'totalitarian'.[1] The more completely public finance can be separated from the regulation of the monetary circulation, the better it will be. It is a power which always has been harmful. Its use for financial purposes is always an abuse. And government has neither the *interest* nor the *capacity* to exercise it in the manner required to secure the smooth flow of economic effort.

*

The suggestion of depriving government of the monopoly of issuing money and of its power of making any money 'legal tender' for all existing debts has been made here in the first instance because governments have invariably and inevitably grossly abused that power throughout the whole of history and thereby gravely disturbed the self-steering mechanism of

---

[1] One alarming feature, the threat of which is not yet sufficiently appreciated, is the spreading tendency to regard a government pension as the *only* trustworthy provision for one's old age, because experience seems to demonstrate that political expediency will force governments to maintain or even to increase its real value.

the market. But it may turn out that cutting off government from the tap which supplies it with additional money for its use may prove as important in order to stop the inherent tendency of unlimited government to grow indefinitely, which is becoming as menacing a danger to the future of civilisation as the badness of the money it has supplied. Only if people are made to perceive that they must pay in undisguised taxes (or voluntarily lend) all the money government can spend can the process of buying majority support by granting special benefits to ever-increasing numbers with particular interests be brought to a stop.

**

XXII. PROBLEMS OF TRANSITION

For the vast majority of people the appearance of several con-current currencies would merely offer them alternatives; it would not make necessary any change in their habitual use of money. Experience would gradually teach them how to improve their position by switching to other kinds of money. Retail merchants would soon be offered by the banks the appropriate calculating equipment which would relieve them of any initial difficulties in management or accounting. Since the issuer of the money they used would be interested in supplying assistance, they would probably discover they were better served than before. In manufacture, trade and the service industries, learning to take full advantage of the new opportunities might take a little longer, but there would be no important necessary changes in the conduct of business or unavoidably difficult adaptations.

Preventing rapid depreciation of formerly exclusive currency
The two activities that would be most profoundly affected, and in which an almost complete change of habitual practices and routines would be required, are public finance and the whole range of private finance, including banking, insurance, building societies, saving and mortgage banks as well. For government, apart from the changes in financial policy mentioned in Section XXI, the chief task would be to guard against a rapid displacement and consequent accelerating depreciation of the currency issued by the existing central bank. This

could probably be achieved only by instantly giving it complete freedom and independence, putting it thus on the same footing with all other issue banks, foreign or newly created at home, coupled with a simultaneous return to a policy of balanced budgets, limited only by the possibility of borrowing on an open loan market which they could not manipulate. The urgency of these steps derives from the fact that, once the displacement of the hitherto exclusive currency by new currencies had commenced, it would be rapidly speeded up by an accelerating depreciation that would be practically impossible to stop by any of the ordinary methods of contracting the circulation. Neither the government nor the former central banks would possess the reserves of other currencies or of gold to redeem all the old money the public would want to get rid of as soon as it could change from a rapidly depreciating currency to one it had reason to believe would remain stable. It could be brought to trust such a currency only if the bank issuing it demonstrated a capacity to regulate it in precisely the same manner as the new issue banks competing with it.

Introduce new currencies at once, not gradually

The other important requirement of government action, if the transition to the new order is to be successful, is that all the required liberties be conceded at once, and no tentative and timid attempt be made to introduce the new order gradually, or to reserve powers of control 'in case anything goes wrong'. The possibility of free competition between a multiplicity of issuing institutions and the complete freedom of all movements of currency and capital across frontiers are equally essential to the success of the scheme. Any hesitant approach by a *gradual* relaxation of the existing monopoly of issue would be certain to make it fail. People would learn to trust the new money only if they were confident it was completely exempt from any government control. Only because they were under the sharp control of competition could the private banks be trusted to keep their money stable. Only because people could freely choose which currency to use for their different purposes would the process of selection lead to the good money prevailing. Only because there was active trading on the currency exchange would the issuing banks be warned to take the required action in time. Only because the frontiers were open to the

movement of currency and capital would there be assurance
of no collusion between local institutions to mismanage the
local currency. And only because there were free commodity
markets would stable average prices mean that the process of
adapting supply to demand was functioning.

Commercial bank change in policy

If the government succeeded in handing over the business of
supplying money to private institutions without the existing
currency collapsing, the chief problem for the individual commercial banks would be to decide whether to try and establish
their own currency, or to select the other currency or currencies
in which they would in future conduct their business. The great
majority clearly would have to be content to do their business
in other currencies. They would thus (Sections XI and XII)
have to practise a kind of '100 per cent banking', and keep a
full reserve against all their obligations payable on demand.

This necessity would probably prove the most far-reaching
change in business practice required by competing currencies.
Since these banks presumably would have to charge substantially for running chequing accounts, they would lose that
business largely to the issuing banks and be reduced to the
administration of less liquid kinds of capital assets.

So long as this change could be effected by a deliberate
transition to the use of a currency of their choice, it might prove
somewhat painful but not raise unmanageable problems. And
to do away with banks which, in effect, created currency
without bearing any responsibility for the results has been for
more than a hundred years the desideratum of economists who
perceived the inherent instability of the mechanism into which
we had drifted but who usually saw no hope of ever getting
out of it. An institution which has proved as harmful as
fractional reserve banking without responsibility of the individual bank for the money (i.e. cheque deposits) it created
cannot complain if the support by a government monopoly
that has made its existence possible is withdrawn. There will
certainly also have to develop generally a much sharper
distinction between pure banking and the investment business,
or between what used to be regarded as the English and the
Continental types of banks (*Depositenbanken* and *Spekulations-
banken* as these types were once described in German). I expect
that it will soon be discovered that the business of creating

money does not go along well with the control of large investment portfolios or even control of large parts of industry.

A wholly different set of difficulties would of course arise if the government or its privileged bank did not succeed in preventing a collapse of its currency. This would be a possibility which the banks not able to issue their own currency would rightly fear, since a large part of their assets, namely all their loans, would dwindle away with most of their liabilities. But this would merely mean that the danger of a high inflation, of the kind that now always threatens and that others might avoid by shifting to other currencies, would for them become particularly threatening. But banks have usually claimed that they have more or less succeeded in bringing their assets through even a galloping inflation. Bankers who do not know how to do it might perhaps consult their colleagues in Chile and elsewhere where they have had plenty of experience with this problem. At any rate, to get rid of the present unstable structure is too important a task for it to be sacrificed to the interests of some special groups.

XXIII. PROTECTION AGAINST THE STATE

Though under the proposed arrangement the normal provision of money would be entirely a function of private enterprise, the chief danger to its smooth working would still be interference by the state.[1] If the international character of the issuing business should largely protect the issuing banks against direct political pressure (though it would certainly invite attacks by demagogues), the trust in any one institution would still largely depend on the trust in the government under which it was established. To obviate the suspicion of serving the political interests of the country in which they were established, it would clearly be important that banks with headquarters in different countries should compete with one another. The greatest confidence, at least so long as peace was regarded as

---

[1] I use here for once the term 'state' because it is the expression which in the context would be commonly used by most people who would wish to emphasise the probability of the beneficial nature of these public activities. Most people rapidly become aware of the idealistic and unrealistic nature of their argument if it is pointed out to them that the agent who acts is never an abstract state but always a very concrete government with all the defects necessarily inherent in this kind of political institution.

assured, would probably be placed in institutions established in small wealthy countries for which international business was an important source of income and that would therefore be expected to be particularly careful of their reputation for financial soundness.

Pressures for return to national monetary monopolies

Many countries would probably try, by subsidies or similar measures, to preserve a locally established bank issuing a distinct national currency that would be available side by side with the international currencies, even if they were only moderately successful. There would then be some danger that the nationalist and socialist forces active in a silly agitation against multinational corporations would lead governments, by advantages conceded to the national institution, to bring about a gradual return to the present system of privileged national issuers of currency.

Recurring governmental control of currency and capital movements

The chief danger, however, would threaten from renewed attempts by governments to control the international movements of currency and capital. It is a power which at present is the most serious threat not only to a working international economy but also to personal freedom; and it will remain a threat so long as governments have the physical power to enforce such controls. It is to be hoped that people will gradually recognise this threat to their personal freedom and that they will make the complete prohibition of such measures an entrenched constitutional provision. The ultimate protection against the tyranny of government is that at least a large number of able people can emigrate when they can no longer stand it. I fear that few Englishmen, most of whom thought the statement which I now repeat unduly alarmist and exaggerated when I published it more than 30 years ago, will still feel so:

'The extent of the control over all life that economic control confers is nowhere better illustrated than in the field of foreign exchanges. Nothing would at first seem to affect private life less than a state control of the dealings in foreign exchange, and most people will regard its introduction with complete indifference. Yet the experience of most continental countries has taught thoughtful people to regard this step as the decisive advance on the path to totalitarianism and the suppression of individual liberty. It is in fact the complete delivery of the individual to the tyranny of the state, the final suppression of all means of escape—not merely for the rich, but for everybody. Once the individual is no longer free to travel, no longer free to buy foreign books or journals, once all means of foreign contact can be restricted to those whom official opinion approves or for whom it is regarded as necessary, the effective control of opinion is much greater than that ever exercised by any of the absolutist governments of the seventeenth and eighteenth centuries.'[1]

Next to the barrier to the excessive growth of government expenditure, the second fundamental contribution to the protection of individual freedom which the abolition of the government monopoly of issuing money would secure would probably be the intertwining of international affairs, which would make it more and more impossible for government to control international movements, and thus safeguard the ability of dissidents to escape the oppression of a government with which they profoundly disagreed.

XXIV. THE LONG-RUN PROSPECTS

A hope one may cherish is that, as competition usually does, it will lead to the discovery of yet unknown possibilities in currency. This makes any attempt at prediction of the long-run effects of the proposed reform exceedingly hazardous, but we will attempt to summarise briefly what would appear to be the probable long-run developments if it were adopted.

I believe that, once the system had fully established itself and competition had eliminated a number of unsuccessful ventures, there would remain in the free world several extensively used and very similar currencies. In various large regions one or two of them would be dominant, but these regions would have no sharp or constant boundaries, and the use of the currencies dominant in them would overlap in broad and fluctuating border districts. Most of these currencies, based on similar

[1] Hayek [28], p. 69, note.

collections of commodities, would in the short run fluctuate very little in terms of one another, probably much less than the currencies of the most stable countries today, yet somewhat more than currencies based on a true gold standard. If the composition of the commodity basket on which they are based were adapted to the conditions of the region in which they are mainly used, they might slowly drift apart. But most of them would thus *concur*, not only in the sense of running side by side, but also in the sense of agreeing with one another in the movement of their values.

After the experimental process of finding the most favoured collection of commodities to the price of which the currency was to be tied, further changes would probably be rare and minor. Competition between the issuing banks would concentrate on the avoidance of even minor fluctuations of their value in terms of these commodities, the degree of information provided about their activities, and various additional services (such as assistance in accounting) offered to their customers. The currencies issued by any surviving government banks would often themselves be driven more and more to accept and even to seek payment in currencies other than those issued by a favoured national institution.

*

The possibility of a multiplicity of similar currencies

There exists, however, a possibility or even probability I did not consider in the First Edition. After certain currencies based on a particular batch of commodities have become widely accepted, many other banks might, under different names, issue currencies the value of which was based on the same collection of commodities as the one successful first, either in the same or smaller or larger units. In other words, competition might lead to the extensive use of the same commodity base by a large number of issue banks that would still compete for the favour of the public through the constancy of the value of their issues or other services they offer. The public might then learn to accept a considerable number of such moneys with different names (but all described as, say, of 'Zurich Standard') at constant rates of exchange; and shops might post lists of all the currencies which they were prepared to accept as representing that standard. So long as the press properly exercised its supervisory function and warned the public in time of any dereliction of duty on the part of some issuers, such a system might satisfactorily serve for a long time.

Considerations of convenience would probably also lead to the adoption of a standard unit, i.e. based not only on the same collection of commodities but also of the same magnitude. In this case most banks could issue, under distinct names, notes for these standard units which would be readily accepted locally as far as the reputation of the individual bank extended.

The preservation of a standard of long-term debts even while currencies may lose their value

With the availability of at least some stable currencies the absurd practice of making 'legal tender' a mere token which may become valueless but still remain effective for the discharge of debts contracted in what had been an object of a certain value is bound to disappear. It was solely the power of government to force upon people what they had not meant in their contracts which produced this absurdity. With the abolition of the government monopoly of issuing money the courts will soon understand, and, I trust, statute law recognise, that justice requires debts to be paid in terms of the units of value which the parties to the contracts intended and not in what government says is a substitute for them. (The exception is where the contract explicitly provides for a stated number of tokens rather than for a value expressed in terms of an amount of tokens.)

After the development of a widely preferred common standard of value the courts would in most cases have no difficulty in determining the approximate magnitude of the abstract value intended by the parties to a contract for the value of such and such an amount of a widely accepted unit of currency. If one currency in terms of the value of which a contract had been concluded seriously depreciated beyond a reasonable range of fluctuation, a court would not allow the parties to gain or lose from the malpractice of the third party that issued the currency. They would without difficulty be able to determine the amount of some other currency or currencies with which the debtor was entitled and obliged to discharge his obligation.

As a result, even the complete collapse of one currency would not have the disastrous far-reaching consequences which a similar event has today. Though the holders of cash, either in the form of notes or of demand deposits in a particular currency, might lose their whole value, this would be a relatively minor disturbance compared with the general shrinkage or wiping out of all claims to third persons expressed in that currency. The whole structure of long-term contracts would remain unaffected, and people would preserve their investments in bonds, mortgages and similar forms of claims even though they might lose all their cash if they were unfortunate to use the currency of a bank that failed. A portfolio of bonds and other long-term claims might still be a very safe investment even if it happened that some issuers of currency became insolvent and their notes and deposits valueless. Completely liquid assets would still involve a risk—but who wants, except perhaps temporarily, to keep all his assets in a very liquid form? There could never occur that complete disappearance of any common standard of debts or such a wiping out of all monetary obligations as has been the final effect of all major inflations. Long before this could happen, everybody would have deserted the depreciated unit and no old obligation could be discharged in terms of it.

*

New legal framework for banking

While governments should not interfere in this development by any conscious attempts at control (i.e. any acts of intervention in the strict sense of the term), it may be found that new rules of law are needed to provide an appropriate legal framework within which the new banking practices could successfully develop. It would, however, seem rather doubtful whether it would assist developments if such rules were at once made generally applicable by international treaties and experimentation with alternative arrangements thereby prevented.

How long it would take for some countries no longer to desire to have a currency of their own for purely nationalistic or prestige reasons, and for governments to stop misleading the public by complaining about an undue restriction of their sovereign power, is difficult to say.[1] The whole system is of course wholly irreconcilable with any striving for totalitarian powers of any sort.

[1] Indeed it would be the day of final triumph of the new system when governments began to prefer to receive taxes in currencies other than those they issue!

[125]

XXV. CONCLUSIONS

The abolition of the government monopoly of money was conceived to prevent the bouts of acute inflation and deflation which have plagued the world for the past 60 years. It proves on examination to be also the much needed cure for a more deep-seated disease: the recurrent waves of depression and unemployment that have been represented as an inherent and deadly defect of capitalism.

Gold standard not the solution

One might hope to prevent the violent fluctuations in the value of money in recent years by returning to the gold standard or some régime of fixed exchanges. I still believe that, *so long as the management of money is in the hands of government*, the gold standard with all its imperfections is the only tolerably safe system. But we certainly can do better than that, though not through government. Quite apart from the undeniable truth that the gold standard also has serious defects, the opponents of such a move can properly point out that a central direction of the quantity of money is in the present circumstances necessary to counteract the inherent instability of the existing credit system. But once it is recognised that this inherent instability of credit is itself the effect of the structure of deposit banking determined by the monopolistic control of the supply of the hand-to-hand money in which the deposits must be redeemed, these objections fall to the ground. If we want free enterprise and a market economy to survive (as even the supporters of a so-called 'mixed economy' presumably also wish), we have no choice but to replace the governmental currency monopoly and national currency systems by free competition between private banks of issue. We have never had the control of money in the hands of agencies whose *sole* and *exclusive* concern was to give the public what currency it liked best among several kinds offered, and which at the same time staked their existence on fulfilling the expectations they had created.

*

It may be that, with free competition between different kinds of money, gold coins might at first prove to be the most popular. But this very fact, the increasing demand for gold, would probably lead to such a rise (and perhaps also violent fluctuations) of the price of gold that, though it might still be widely used for hoarding, it would soon cease to be convenient as the unit for business transactions and accounting. There should certainly be the same freedom for its use, but I should not expect this to lead to its victory over other forms of privately issued money, the demand for which rested on its quantity being successfully regulated so as to keep its purchasing power constant.

The very same fact which at present makes gold more trusted than government-controlled paper money, namely that its total quantity cannot be manipulated at will in the service of political aims, would in the long run make it appear inferior to token money used by competing institutions whose business rested on successfully so regulating the quantity of their issues as to keep the value of the units approximately constant.

**

Good money can come only from self-interest, not from benevolence

We have always had bad money because private enterprise was not permitted to give us a better one. In a world governed by the pressure of organised interests, the important truth to keep in mind is that we cannot count on intelligence or understanding but only on sheer self-interest to give us the institutions we need. Blessed indeed will be the day when it will no longer be from the benevolence of the government that we expect good money but from the regard of the banks for their own interest.

'It is in this manner that we obtain from one another the far greater part of those good offices we stand in need of'[1]

—but unfortunately not yet a money that we can rely upon.

It was not 'capitalism' but government intervention which has been responsible for the recurrent crises of the past.[2] Government has prevented enterprise from equipping itself with the instruments that it required to protect itself against its efforts being misdirected by an unreliable money and that it would be both profitable for the supplier and beneficial to all others to develop. The recognition of this truth makes it clear that the reform proposed is not a minor technicality of finance

[1] Adam Smith [54], p. 26.
[2] A theme repeatedly argued by the late Ludwig von Mises [45-47].

but a crucial issue which may decide the fate of free civilisation. What is proposed here seems to me the only discernible way of completing the market order and freeing it from its main defect and the cause of the chief reproaches directed against it.

Is competitive paper currency practicable?

We cannot, of course, hope for such a reform before the public understands what is at stake and what it has to gain. But those who think the whole proposal wholly impracticable and utopian should remember that 200 years ago in *The Wealth of Nations* Adam Smith wrote that

'to expect, indeed, that the freedom of trade should ever be entirely restored in Great Britain, is as absurd as to expect that an Oceana or Utopia should ever be established in it'.[1]

It took nearly 90 years from the publication of his work in 1776 until Great Britain became the first country to establish complete free trade in 1860. But the idea caught on rapidly; and if it had not been for the political reaction caused by the French Revolution and the Napoleonic Wars no doubt it would have taken effect much sooner. It was not until 1819 that an effective movement to educate the general public on these matters started and it was in the end due to the devoted efforts of a few men who dedicated themselves to spread the message by an organised Free Trade Movement that what Smith had called 'the insolent outrage of furious and disappointed monopolists' was overcome.[2,3]

[1] [54], p. 471. The whole paragraph beginning with the sentence quoted and concluding with the phrase cited further on is well worth reading in the present connection.

[2] As a reviewer of the First Edition of this essay (John Porteous, *New Statesman*, 14 January, 1977) sensibly observed: 'It would have seemed unthinkable 400 years ago that governments would ever relinquish control over religious belief.'

[3] It has been said that my suggestion to 'construct' wholly new monetary institutions is in conflict with my general philosophical attitude. But nothing is further from my thoughts than any wish to design new institutions. What I propose is simply to remove the existing obstacles which for ages have prevented the evolution of desirable institutions in money. Our monetary and banking system is the product of harmful restrictions imposed by governments to increase their powers. They are certainly not institutions of which it can said they have been tried and found good, since the people were not allowed to try any alternative.

To justify the demand for freedom of development in this field it was necessary to explain what consequences would probably result from granting such freedom. But what it is possible to foresee is necessarily limited. It is one of the great merits of freedom that it encourages new inventions, and they are in their very nature

[Contd. on page 129]

*

I fear that since 'Keynesian' propaganda has filtered through to the masses, has made inflation respectable and provided agitators with arguments which the professional politicians are unable to refute, the only way to avoid being driven by continuing inflation into a controlled and directed economy, and therefore ultimately in order to save civilisation, will be to deprive governments of their power over the supply of money.[1]

** **

'Free Money Movement'

What we now need is a Free Money Movement comparable to the Free Trade Movement of the 19th century, demonstrating not merely the harm caused by acute inflation, which could justifiably be argued to be avoidable even with present institutions, but the deeper effects of producing periods of stagnation that are indeed inherent in the present monetary arrangements.

The alarm about current inflation is, as I can observe as I write, only too quickly dispelled whenever the rate of inflation slows down only a little. I have not much doubt that, by the time these lines appear in print, there will be ample cause for a renewal of this alarm (unless, which would be even worse, the resumed inflation is concealed by price controls). Probably even the new inflationary boom already initiated will again have collapsed. But it will need deeper insight into the superficially invisible effects of inflation to produce the result required to achieve the abolition of the harmful powers of

[Contd. from page 128]
unpredictable. I expect evolution to be much more inventive than I can possibly be. Though it is always the new ideas of comparatively few which shape social evolution, the difference between a free and a regulated system is precisely that in the former it is people who have the better ideas who will determine developments because they will be imitated, while in the latter only the ideas and desires of those in power are allowed to shape evolution. Freedom always creates some new risks. All I can say is that if I were responsible for the fate of a country dear to me I would gladly take that risk in the field I have been considering here.

[1] Recent experience also suggests that in future governments may find themselves exposed to international pressure to pursue monetary policies which, while harmful to their own citizens, are supposed to help some other country, and will be able to escape such pressure only by divesting themselves both of the power and the responsibility of controlling the supply of money. We have already reached a stage in which countries which have succeeded in reducing the annual rate of *inflation* to 5 per cent are exhorted by others who lustily continue to inflate at 15 per cent per annum to assist them by 'reflation'.

government on the control of money. There is thus an immense educational task ahead before we can hope to free ourselves from the gravest threat to social peace and continued prosperity inherent in existing monetary institutions.

*

It will be necessary that the problem and the urgent need of reform come to be widely understood. The issue is not one which, as may at first appear to the layman, concerns a minor technicality of the financial system which he has never quite understood. It refers to the one way in which we may still hope to stop the continuous progress of all government towards totalitarianism which already appears to many acute observers as inevitable. I wish I could advise that we proceed slowly. But the time may be short. What is now urgently required is not the construction of a new system but the prompt removal of all the legal obstacles which have for two thousand years blocked the way for an evolution which is bound to throw up beneficial results which we cannot now foresee.

**

QUESTIONS FOR DISCUSSION

1. Examine the long-held view that there should be only one currency in a country and that it should be controlled by government. Illustrate your discussion with examples from remote and recent history.

2. What are the origins of legal tender? Argue for and against it as the necessary basis of a monetary system.

3. Define money. How is it distinguished from non-money? Argue for and against the concept of a 'quantity' of money. Apply the argument to the 'quantity' theory of money.

4. 'It is desirable for government to control money so that it can vary its supply according to the needs of the economy.' 'People have been losing confidence in money because it has been controlled by government.' Discuss.

5. History shows that there has sometimes been lack of confidence in 'legal tender' paper currencies. How could a régime of competing paper currencies maintain the confidence of the public?

6. 'To be trusted, paper money must be convertible into valuable goods or precious metals.' Do you agree? Discuss the condition in which convertibility is and is not essential.

7. Discuss the view that inflation and deflation would be difficult or impossible if the quantity of money were not controlled by government. Illustrate your answer from the 1929-32 Great Depression and the 1972-75 'Great Inflation'.

8. Boom and slump are associated with 'capitalism'. Are they found in non-capitalist economies? Are they the result of capitalism or other causes?

9. 'It is politically impossible for a monetary authority subject or exposed to severe sectional pressures to avoid increasing the quantity of money to increase employment, thus creating inflation. The gold standard, fixed exchange rates and other restraints in the way of monetary expansion have been found inadequate.' Discuss.

10. How would you remove the power of national government to control the international movement of currency? Would international agreement suffice? How could competition in currency be more effective?

A.S.

THE DESTRUCTION OF PAPER MONEY,
1950-1975

Country	Percentage Decline in Purchasing Power	Percentage Increase in Cost-of- Living	Percentage Change in Free or Black Market Value*
Chile	99	11,318,874	−99
Uruguay	99	323,173	−99
Argentina	99	196,675	−99
Brazil	99	61,000	−99
Bolivia	99	50,792	−99
Korea, South	99	37,935	−47
Viet Nam	99	n.a.	n.a.
Paraguay	97	3,058	−86
Iceland	95	1,789	−91
Israel	94	1,684	−93
Colombia	93	1,262	−91
Turkey	91	997	−77
Peru	90	907	−78
Yugoslavia	90	870	−75
Taiwan	89	848	−73
Ghana	85	587	−63
Spain	82	466	−16
Mexico	80	404	−31
Finland	79	374	+29
Ireland	78	363	−23
Japan	78	362	+39
United Kingdom	78	345	−20
Greece	76	314	−51
France	75	305	−13
Denmark	74	282	+56
Portugal	74	279	−26
India	73	275	−41
Norway	73	272	+73
Philippines	73	272	−59

*Vis-à-vis the US Dollar.

Source: Reprinted with permission of the author and publisher from Franz Pick, Pick's Currency Yearbook: 1976-77 Edition, Pick Publishing Corporation, New York, 1977.

Appendix: The Destruction of Paper Money (continued)

Country	Percentage Decline in Purchasing Power	Percentage Increase in Cost-of-Living	Percentage Change in Free or Black Market Value*
Iran	73	271	−22
Sudan	73	270	n.a.
Ecuador	73	267	−29
New Zealand	73	266	−19
Australia	73	265	+30
Sweden	72	261	+38
Burma	72	257	n.a.
Italy	72	253	−6
Austria	71	243	+71
Netherlands	68	216	+52
Costa Rica	67	207	−6
Thailand	67	207	+ 4
South Africa	67	204	−16
Syria	66	191	−6
Tunisia	62	160	n.a.
Belgium	61	155	+26
Canada	59	142	+3
Dominican Republic	58	136	−22
Switzerland	57	133	+63
United States	57	131	−75**
El Salvador	57	130	−17
Germany, West	53	115	+110
Egypt	52	107	−41
Sri Lanka	51	103	−61
Iraq	49	95	+11
Malaysia	47	87	+39
Venezuela	45	82	−22
Guatemala	44	77	−
Panama	40	66	−

*Vis-à-vis the US Dollar.
**Depreciation in terms of gold, based on US $141·00 per ounce free market gold price at end of 1975 vs. US $35·00 per ounce official price in 1950.

BIBLIOGRAPHY

(Including some relevant works not explicitly referred to in the text.)

For reprints or translations, square brackets show the year of original publication, but page references are to the later publication quoted in full.

[1] Archibald Alison, *History of Europe*, vol. I, London, 1833.

[2] Joseph Aschheim and Y. S. Park, *Artificial Currency Units: The Formation of Functional Currency Areas*, Essays in International Finance, No. 114, Princeton, 1976.

[3] Walter Bagehot, *Lombard Street* [1873], Kegan Paul, London, 1906.

[4] Paul Barth, *Die Philosophie der Geschichte als Soziologie*, 2nd edn., Leipzig, 1915.

[5] Jean Bodin, *The Six Books of a Commonweale* [1576], London, 1606.

[5a] Fernand Braudel, *Capitalism and the Material Life 1400-1800* [1967], London, 1973.

[6] S. P. Breckinridge, *Legal Tender*, University of Chicago Press, Chicago, 1903.

[7] C. Bresciani-Turroni, *The Economics of Inflation* [1931], Allen & Unwin, London, 1937.

[7a] Henry Phelps Brown and Sheila V. Hopkins, 'Seven Centuries of the Prices of Consumables, compared with Builders' Wage-rates', *Economica*, November 1956.

[7b] Henry Phelps Brown and Sheila V. Hopkins, 'Builders' Wage-rates, Prices and Population: Some Further Evidence', *Economica*, February 1959.

[8] W. W. Carlile, *The Evolution of Modern Money*, Macmillan, London, 1901.

[9] H. Cernuschi, *Mecanique de l'echange*, Paris, 1865.

[10] H. Cernuschi, *Contre le billet de banques*, Paris, 1866.

[11] Carlo M. Cipolla, *Money, Prices and Civilization in the Mediterranean World: Fifth to Seventeenth Century*, Gordian Press, New York, 1967.

[12] Lauchlin Currie, *The Supply and Control of Money in the United States*, Harvard University Press, Cambridge, Mass., 1934.

[12a] Raymond de Roover, *Gresham on Foreign Exchanges*, Cambridge, Mass., 1949.

[13] C. H. Douglas, *Social Credit* [1924], Omnie Publications, Hawthorn, Calif., 1966.

[14] Otto Eckstein, 'Instability in the Private and Public Sector', *Swedish Journal of Economics*, 75/1, 1973.

[15] Wilhelm Endemann, *Studien in der Romanisch-kanonistischen Rechtslehre*, vol. II, Berlin, 1887.

[16] A. E. Feaveryear, *The Pound Sterling*, Oxford University Press, London, 1931.

[17] Lord Farrer, *Studies in Currency*, London, 1898.

[17a] F. W. Fetter, 'Some Neglected Aspects of Gresham's Law', *Quarterly Journal of Economics*, XLVI, 1931/2.

[18] Stanley Fischer, 'The Demand for Index Bonds', *Journal of Political Economy*, 83/3, 1975.

[18a] Ferdinand Friedensburg, *Münzkunde und Geldgeschichte des Mittelalters und der Neuzeit*, Munich and Berlin, 1926.

[19] Milton Friedman, 'Commodity Reserve Currency' [1951], in *Essays in Positive Economics*, University of Chicago Press, Chicago, 1953.

[20] Milton Friedman, *A Program for Monetary Stability*, Fordham University Press, New York, 1960.

[20a] Milton Friedman, 'The Quantity Theory of Money: A Restatement', in *Studies in the Quantity Theory of Money*, Chicago, 1956.

[20b] Milton Friedman, *Monetary Correction*, Occasional Paper 41, Institute of Economic Affairs, London, 1974.

[21] Josef Garnier, *Traité théorique et pratique du change et des operation de banque*, Paris, 1841.

[21a] Richard Gaettens, *Inflationen, Das Drama der Geldentwertungen vom Altertum bis zur Gegenwart*, Munich, 1955.

[22] Silvio Gesell, *The Natural Economic Order* [1916], Rev. Edn., Peter Owen, London, 1958.

[22a] Herbert Giersch, 'On the Desirable Degree of Flexibility of Exchange Rates', *Weltwirtschaftliches Archiv*, CIX, 1973.

[23] H. Grote, *Die Geldlehre*, Leipzig, 1865.

[23a] R. F. Harrod, *The Life of John Maynard Keynes*, London, 1951.

[24] F. A. Hayek, *Prices and Production*, Routledge, London, 1931.

[25] F. A. Hayek, *Monetary Theory and the Trade Cycle* [1929], Jonathan Cape, London, 1933.

[26] F. A. Hayek, 'Über "Neutrales Geld" ', *Zeitschrift für Nationalökonomie*, 4/5, 1933.

[27] F. A. Hayek, *Monetary Nationalism and International Stability*, The Graduate School of International Studies, Geneva, 1937.

[28] F. A. Hayek, *The Road to Serfdom*, Routledge, London and Chicago, 1944.

[29] F. A. Hayek, *The Constitution of Liberty*, Routledge & Kegan Paul, London and Chicago, 1960.

[30] F. A. Hayek, *Studies in Philosophy, Politics and Economics*, Routledge & Kegan Paul, London and Chicago, 1967.

[31] F. A. Hayek, *Choice in Currency*, Occasional Paper 48, Institute of Economic Affairs, London, 1976.

[31a] F. A. Hayek, *Law, Legislation and Liberty*, Routledge & Kegan Paul and the University of Chicago Press, London and Chicago, vol. I, 1973, vol. II, 1976, vol. III forthcoming.

[31b] Karl Helfferich, 'Die geschichtliche Entwicklung der Münzsysteme', *Jahrbücher für Nationalökonomie*, 3.f. IX (LXIV), 1895.

[32] Marianne von Herzfeld, 'Die Geschichte als Funktion der Geldwertbewegungen', *Archiv für Sozialwissenschaft und Sozialpolitik*, 56/3, 1926.

[33] J. R. Hicks, 'A Suggestion for Simplifying the Theory of Money', *Economica*, February 1935.

[34] W. S. Jevons, *Money and the Mechanism of Exchange*, Kegan Paul, London, 1875.

[34a] H. G. Johnson, *Essays in Monetary Economics* [1967], Second Edition, London, 1969.

[34b] H. G. Johnson, *Further Essays in Monetary Economics*, London, 1972.

[34c] H. G. Johnson and A. K. Swoboda (eds.), *The Economics of Common Currencies*, London, 1973.

[34d] Robert A. Jones, 'The Origin and Development of Media of Exchange', *Journal of Political Economy*, LXXXIV, 1976.

[35] Benjamin Klein, 'The Competitive Supply of Money', *Journal of Money, Credit and Banking*, VI, November 1975.

[35a] Benjamin Klein, 'Competing Moneys: Comment', *Journal of Money, Credit and Banking*, 1975.

[36] G. F. Knapp, *The State Theory of Money* [1905], Macmillan, London, 1924.

[37] Axel Leijonhufvud, *On Keynesian Economics and the Economics of Keynes*, Oxford University Press, New York and London, 1968.

[37a] Wilhelm Lexis, 'Bermerkungen über Paralellgeld und Sortengeld', *Jahrbücher für Nationalökonomie*, 3.f.IX (LXIV), 1895.

[37b] Thelma Liesner & Mervyn A. King (eds.), *Indexing for Inflation*, London, 1975.

[37c] R. G. Lipsey, 'Does Money Always Depreciate?', *Lloyds Bank Review*, 58, October 1960.

[38] S. J. Loyd (later Lord Overstone), *Further Reflections on the State of the Currency and the Action of the Bank of England*, London, 1837.

[137]

[39] Fritz Machlup, 'Euro-Dollar Creation: A Mystery Story', *Banca Nazionale del Lavoro Quarterly Review*, 94, 1970, reprinted Princeton, December 1970.

[40] R. I. McKinnon, 'Optimum Currency Areas', *American Economic Review*, 53/4, 1963.

[41] F. A. Mann, *The Legal Aspects of Money*, 3rd Edition, Oxford University Press, London, 1971.

[42] Arthur W. Marget, *The Theory of Prices*, 2 vols., Prentice-Hall, New York and London, 1938 and 1942.

[42a] A. James Meigs, *Money Matters*, Harper & Row, New York, 1972.

[43] Carl Menger, *Principles of Economics* [1871], The Free Press, Glencoe, Ill., 1950.

[43a] Carl Menger, 'Geld' [1892], *Collected Works of Carl Menger*, ed. by the London School of Economics, London, 1934.

[44] Henry Meulen, *Free Banking*, 2nd Edition, Macmillan, London, 1934.

[44a] Fritz W. Meyer and Alfred Schüller, *Spontane Ordnungen in der Geldwirtschaft und das Inflationsproblem*, Tübingen, 1976.

[45] Ludwig von Mises, *The Theory of Money and Credit* [1912], New Edition, Jonathan Cape, London, 1952.

[46] Ludwig von Mises, *Geldwertstabilisierung und Konjunkturpolitik*, Jena, 1928.

[47] Ludwig von Mises, *Human Action*, William Hodge, Edinburgh, 1949; Henry Regnery, Chicago, 1966.

[47a] E. Victor Morgan, *A History of Money* [1965], Penguin Books, Hardmondsworth, Rev. Edition, 1969.

[48] Robert A. Mundell, 'The International Equilibrium', *Kyklos*, 14, 1961.

[49] Robert A. Mundell, 'A Theory of Optimum Currency Areas', *American Economic Review*, 51, September 1963.

[49a] W. T. Newlyn, 'The Supply of Money and Its Content', *Economic Journal*, LXXIV, 1964.

[50] Arthur Nussbaum, *Money in the Law, National and International*, Foundation Press, Brooklyn, 1950.

[50a] Karl Olivecrona, *The Problem of the Monetary Unit*, Stockholm, 1957.

[50b] Franz Pick and René Sédillot, *All the Moneys of the World. A Chronicle of Currency Values*, Pick Publishing Corporation, New York, 1971.

[50c] Henri Pirenne, *La civilisation occidentale au Moyen Âge du Milieu du XVe siècle*, Paris, 1933.

[51] H. Rittershausen, *Der Neubau des deutschen Kredit-Systems*, Berlin, 1932.

[51a] Herbert Rittmann, *Deutsche Geldgeschichte 1484-1914*, Munich, 1974.

[52] Murray N. Rothbard, *What has Government Done to Our Money?*, New Rev. Edition, Rampart College Publications, Santa Anna, Calif., 1974.

[53] Gasparo Scaruffi, *L'Alitinonfo per far ragione e concordanza d'oro e d'argento*, Reggio, 1582.

[53a] W. A. Shaw, *The History of Currency 1252-1894*, London, 1894.

[54] Adam Smith, *An Inquiry into the Nature and Causes of the Wealth of Nations* [1776], Glasgow edition, Oxford University Press, London, 1976.

[55] Vera C. Smith, *Rationale of Central Banking*, P. S. King, London, 1936.

[56] Werner Sombart, *Der moderne Kapitalismus*, vol. II, 2nd Edition, Munich and Leipzig, 1916/17.

[57] Herbert Spencer, *Social Statics* [1850], Abridged and Rev. Edition, Williams & Norgate, London, 1902.

[58] Wolfgang Stützel, *Über unsere Währungsverfassung*, Tübingen, 1975.

[58a] Brian Summers, 'Private Coinage in America', *The Freeman*, July 1976.

[58b] Earl A. Thompson, 'The Theory of Money and Income Consistent with Orthodox Value Theory', in P. A. Samuelson and G. Horwich (eds.), *Trade, Stability and Macro-economics. Essays in Honor of Lloyd Metzler*, Academic Press, New York and London, 1974.

[59] Gordon Tullock, 'Paper Money—A Cycle in Cathay', *Economic History Review*, IX/3, 1956.

[60] Gordon Tullock, 'Competing Moneys', *Money Credit and Banking*, 1976.

[61] Roland Vaubel, 'Plans for a European Parallel Currency and SDR Reform', *Weltwirtschaftliches Archiv*, 110/2, 1974.

[61a] Roland Vaubel, 'Freier Wettbewerb zwischen Währungen', *Wirtschaftsdienst*, August 1976.

[62] Willem Vissering, *On Chinese Currency. Coin and Paper Money*, Leiden, 1877.

[63] Knut Wicksell, *Geldzins und Güterpreise*, Jena, 1898.

[64] Knut Wicksell, *Vorlesungen über Nationalökonomie* [1922], English Edition, *Lectures on Political Economy*, vol. II: *Money*, Routledge, 1935.

[64a] Leland B. Yeager, 'Essential Properties of the Medium of Exchange', *Kyklos*, 21, 1968.

F. A. Hayek's Principal Writings
Published in English

Prices and Production, Routledge & Kegan Paul, 1931.

Monetary Theory and the Trade Cycle, Jonathan Cape, 1933.

Monetary Nationalism and International Stability, Longmans, 1937.

Profits, Interest and Investment, Routledge & Kegan Paul, 1939.

The Pure Theory of Capital, Routledge & Kegan Paul, 1941.

The Road to Serfdom, 1944.*

Individualism and Economic Order, 1948 (Germany 1952).*

John Stuart Mill and Harriet Taylor, 1951.*

The Sensory Order, 1952.*

The Counter-Revolution of Science, The Free Press, Glencoe, Ill., 1955.

The Political Ideal of the Rule of Law, Cairo, 1955.

The Constitution of Liberty, 1960.*

Studies in Philosophy, Politics and Economics, 1967.*

Law, Legislation and Liberty:
  Vol. I: *Rules and Order,* 1973.*
  Vol. II: *The Mirage of Social Justice,* 1976.*
  Vol. III: *The Political Order of a Free Society* (forthcoming).*

---

* Published by Routledge & Kegan Paul, London, and University of Chicago Press, Chicago, Ill.

IEA Papers by F. A. Hayek

Occasional Paper 48
CHOICE IN CURRENCY
A Way to Stop Inflation
with Commentaries by
IVOR F. PEARCE, HAROLD B. ROSE, DOUGLAS JAY, MP, and SIR KEITH JOSEPH, MP
1976   2nd Impression 1977   £1·00
'The idea of repealing the legal tender laws so that people could carry out business in dollars, marks, ounces of gold, EEC "Europas", or anything else may seem removed from everyday experience. But before long it will be necessary to take it very seriously indeed.'

Samuel Brittan, *Financial Times*

Occasional Paper 45
FULL EMPLOYMENT AT ANY PRICE?
Three lectures by the 1974 Nobel Laureate
including his Nobel Memorial Prize Lecture
1975   3rd Impression 1976   £1·00
'The nature of the dilemma has been analysed brilliantly . . . Professor Hayek's analysis deserves a wider readership than professional economists. The problem he is discussing could be a life or death matter to our society.'

Ronald Butt, *The Times*

Occasional Paper 39
ECONOMIC FREEDOM AND REPRESENTATIVE GOVERNMENT
Fourth Wincott Memorial Lecture
1973   2nd Impression 1976   50p
'. . . stated with infuriating reasonableness!'

Economist

Hobart Paperback 4
A TIGER BY THE TAIL
The Keynesian legacy of inflation
1972   2nd Edition 1978   £1·50
'So long, Professor Hayek warns, as trade unions have sufficient monopoly bargaining power to distort pay differentials from their market values, so long will accelerating inflation be the price of the pursuit of full employment.'

Peter Jay, *The Times*

Occasional Paper 20
THE CONFUSION OF LANGUAGE IN POLITICAL THOUGHT
1968   2nd Impression 1976   50p
'Professor Hayek is engaged in a study of the relations between law, legislation and liberty and has found that "serious discussion has been vitiated by the ambiguity of the key terms". The purpose of this paper is to suggest new directions and new terms that would permit a more precise analysis.'

Economic Journal

Some IEA Papers on
Aspects of the New Economics of Politics

Occasional Paper 51

Inflation and Unemployment: The New Dimension of Politics
MILTON FRIEDMAN

1977   2nd Impression 1978   £1·00

'I have to warn you that there is neither shock nor horror nor sensation in his lecture, only close reasoning, and a sense of scholarly inquiry . . . I urge readers to buy and read [it].'
Patrick Hutber, *Sunday Telegraph*

Hobart Paperback 10

Not from benevolence . . .
Twenty years of economic dissent
RALPH HARRIS and ARTHUR SELDON

1977   2nd Impression 1977   £2·00

'If one is to hazard a guess about which organisation has had the greatest influence on public economic understanding, it would not be any of the large forecasting organisations with computer models of the economy, but the Institute of Economic Affairs . . .'
Samuel Brittan, *Financial Times*

Hobart Paperback 9

The Vote Motive
GORDON TULLOCK
with a Commentary by Morris Perlman

1976   £1·50

'Professor Tullock's tract deserves our attention because it is disturbing, as it is meant to be. It invites us to consider further what we should be constantly considering—those comfortable assumptions about our institutions that prompt us to shy away from changes that might be beneficial. There is more in common between the public and private sectors than most of us are willing to allow.'
Municipal Journal

Hobart Paperback 5
Bureaucracy: Servant or Master?
WILLIAM A. NISKANEN
**with Commentaries by
Douglas Houghton, Maurice Kogan,
Nicholas Ridley and Ian Senior**
1973   £1·00
'Niskanen argues, with some cogency, that every kind of pressure on a bureau head leads him to maximise his budget.'
Peter Wilsher, *Sunday Times*

Hobart Paperback 1
Politically Impossible . . .?
W. H. HUTT
1971   75p
'The analysis that Hutt offers is a refreshing and succinct attempt to identify the economic consequences of present trends in welfare expenditure, and the political temptations and attractions he thinks are offered by the alternative policies available. He lives up to the strict standards he suggests for his fellow economists in the earlier section of the book.'
John Biffen, *Spectator*

Occasional Paper 10
Markets and the Franchise
T. W. HUTCHISON
1966   25p
'Professor Hutchison follows the course of electoral reform and its effect on economic ideas. He argues that we need to know a lot more about how people's ideas and wants are translated (or not) into political action, and that in any case we need better mechanisms for collective choice.'   *Investors Chronicle*

Readings 11
E. G. WEST
'"Pure" versus "Operational" Economics in Regional Policy'
in **Regional Policy For Ever?**
Graham Hallett, Peter Randall, E. G. West
1973   £1·80
'. . . to be welcomed for its appraisal of some of the misconceptions that have grown up around the subject.'   *Estates Gazette*

Summary of

Denationalisation of Money

F. A. HAYEK

1. The government monopoly of money must be abolished to stop the recurring bouts of acute inflation and deflation that have become accentuated during the last 60 years.

2. Abolition is also the cure for the more deep-seated disease of the recurring waves of depression and unemployment attributed to 'capitalism'.

3. The monopoly of money by government has relieved it of the need to keep its expenditure within its revenue and has thus precipitated the spectacular increase in government expenditure over the last 30 years.

4. Abolition of the monopoly of money would make it increasingly impossible for government to restrict the international movement of men, money and capital that safeguard the ability of dissidents to escape oppression.

5. These four defects—inflation, instability, undisciplined state expenditure, economic nationalism—have a common origin and a common cure: the replacement of the government monopoly of money by competition in currency supplied by private issuers who, to preserve public confidence, will limit the quantity of their paper issue and thus maintain its value. This is the 'denationalisation of money'.

6. Money does not have to be 'created' legal tender by government: like law, language and morals it can emerge spontaneously. Such 'private' money has often been preferred to government money, but government has usually soon suppressed it.

7. So long as money is managed by government, a gold standard, despite its imperfections, is the only tolerably safe system; but it is better to take money completely out of the control of government.

8. In a world governed by pressures of organised interests, we cannot count on benevolence, intelligence or understanding but only on sheer self-interest to give us the institutions we want. The insight and wisdom of Adam Smith stand today.

9. The proposal is not a minor technicality of finance but a crucial reform that may decide the fate of free civilisation.

10. The urgency of competition in currency requires to be demonstrated to the public by a Free Money Movement, comparable to the Free Trade Movement of the 19th century.

Hobart Paper Special 70 Second Edition is published (price £2.00) by

THE INSTITUTE OF ECONOMIC AFFAIRS
2 Lord North Street, Westminster
London SW1P 3LB   Telephone: 01-799 3745

IEA PUBLICATIONS

Subscription Service

An annual subscription is the most convenient way to obtain our publications. Every title we produce in our regular series will be sent to you immediately on publication and without further charge, representing a substantial saving.

Subscription rates

Britain: £10.00 p.a. including postage, reduced to £9.50 p.a. if paid by Banker's Order.

£7.50 p.a. to students and also to teachers who pay *personally*. No reduction for Banker's Orders.

Europe: 30 US dollars or equivalent.

North America: 35 US dollars.

Other countries: Rates on application. In many countries subscriptions are handled by local agents.

These rates are *not* available to companies or to institutions.

....

To: The Treasurer,
    Institute of Economic Affairs,
    2 Lord North Street,
    Westminster, London SW1P 3LB.

I should like an individual subscription beginning ....
I enclose a cheque/postal order for:

☐ £10.00
☐ £7.50 [student/teacher at ....]
☐ Please send me a Banker's Order form
☐ Please send me an Invoice

Name..

Address ....

              ....

Signed....................................   Date.................